In the spirit of celebrating the proud heritage of Essex County and its people, Broad National Bank is extremely pleased to be the corporate sponsor for Remembering Essex: A Pictorial History of Essex County, New Jersey.

As we mark our own seventy-year anniversary of banking service to our communities, Broad National is especially proud to be playing a leading role in commemorating the colorful saga of the county we call home.

This extensive editorial and photographic account reminds us that our diverse roots are precious legacies which connect us to the present—and to each other—while providing the framework for a bright and prosperous future.

We dedicate this definitive volume not only to those who have helped create the firm foundation of Essex County, but also to the future generations who will continue to build upon and strengthen it.

Donald M. Karp

Chairman and Chief Executive Officer

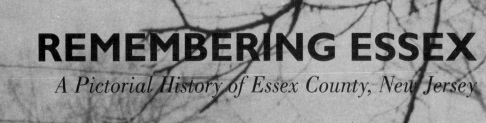

REMEMBERING ESSEX

A Pictorial History of Essex County, New Jersey

By John T. Cunningham and
Charles F. Cummings

THE **DONNING COMPANY** PUBLISHERS

Endsheet photo: Newark Public Library, on its way to becoming one of America's finest small city libraries in 1915, had as its closest neighbor a dying symbol of the past—Bull's Head Stables, where regular horse auctions provided startling contrast with automobiles that were just emerging. Courtesy of Newark Public Library.

Title page photo: Mists rising from icy winter pavements in about 1885 nearly obscured the aging Essex County Courthouse that was built in 1837. Horse-drawn streetcars plodded up "courthouse hill," accompanied by carriages and drays. The courthouse would be replaced in 1907. By then, horsedrawn streetcars were an anomaly that had been replaced by electrically driven trolleys. Courtesy the Newark Public Library.

The Donning Company/Publishers
184 Business Park Drive, Suite 106
Virginia Beach, VA 23462

Steve Mull, General Manager
Debra Y. Quesnel, Project Director
Tracey Emmons-Schneider, Research Coordinator
Mary Jo Kurten, Editor
L. J. Wiley, Art Director, Designer
Dawn V. Kofroth, Production Manager
Tony Lillis, Director of Marketing

Library of Congress Cataloging-in-Publication Data

Cunningham, John T.
Remembering Essex : a pictorial history of Essex County, New Jersey/
by John T. Cunningham and Charles F. Cummings.
p. cm.
Includes bibliographical references (p.   ) and index.
ISBN 0-89865-949-3 (alk. paper)
1. Essex County (N.J.)—History—Pictorial works.
I. Cummings, Charles F. II. Title.
F142.E8C86 1995
974.9'31—dc20
95-35729
CIP

Printed in the United States of America

CONTENTS

No corner in Essex County ever has been more vital than Newark's Broad and Market, where the city and surrounding county were begun in May 1666. It is also unlikely that any photograph of about 1895 more clearly portrayed a Victorian city poised on radical transformation. This elaborately festooned office of the Fireman's Insurance Company on the instant of this shot overlooked a corner where a team of oxen (real, not staged) pulled a cart, horsepower was still genuine, and modest ladies scraped up street dirt with their long skirts. Fifteen years later the old building had yielded to the insurance company's sixteen-story "skyscraper" (first in Newark), oxen and horses had given way to horsepower that drank gasoline, and women's skirts, while not daring, no longer swept the cobblestones. Courtesy the Newark Public Library.

ssex County deserves remembering, not to glorify a vanishing past, but to visualize again the rural, pristine years when meadows were green and clean, when picturesque waterwheels powered scores of gristmills and when streets in the best of villages challenged the ingenuity and good nature of villagers and travelers alike.

Essex deserves memorializing, too, for what it is today. The county is urban now, according to the Census reckoning, but raw figures are never the entire story. Newark and its contiguous communities are urban beyond question, and the marks of urban life reach out along the fingers of avenues called Bloomfield, Central, Springfield, and Mt. Pleasant, stretching to nurture the suburbs.

Statistics and even the views from automobile windows can be misleading. Large patches of green are nearly everywhere in the county, thanks to the formation in 1895 of the nation's first county park system. The view from Eagle Rock eastward, a recurring chord in this book, offers a reassuring panorama of green treetops roofing over densely populated streets. "Urban" and "despair" were never meant to be synonyms.

But remembering is more than bird's-eye views. Our goal is

7

to recall Essex through the eyes and the achievements of artists, etchers, painters, and photographers. Their pens, their brushes, and their cameras have stopped time in its flight, providing the essential structure of *Remembering Essex*.

Thus a water colorist depicted for us a pre-Revolutionary War citizen trudging along rutted Broad Street in the shadow of Trinity Church. Other artists looked eastward from First or Second Mountain or stood before easels in the meadows to capture golden vistas. A few filled canvases with bits of western Essex. Pen-and-ink artists from the popular nineteenth-century illustrated "news weeklies" recorded such events as the State Fair at Waverly, the excited tobogganners at Orange, and the glittering social set at nineteenth-century tennis matches.

Yet for all their artistry, the painters and sketchers could not match the raw reality of photographers, whose skills began to emerge on the big glass plates of the 1870s. Their abilities attained startling competence during the 1890s. Photography became an art in itself.

"Old" photos seem more exciting than most modern ones, chiefly because of the uniqueness of costumes, facial adornment, hats (particularly women's), and backgrounds of nineteenth-century buildings and scenes that have disappeared. Paradoxically, such photos are enhanced by the photographic restraints of seventy-five to one hundred years ago. With very slow film speeds and lenses that were little more than "peepholes" to let in light, even subjects supposedly at play were forced into rigid grim-faced formality.

Cameramen help us "remember" slices of life: four Montclair cyclists but only three bicycles; a Bloomfield couple posed by a tree whose trunk seems only thin bark; the startlingly magnificent old Fireman's Insurance Company headquarters at Broad and Market Streets in Newark, just before it was demolished in the name of progress (meaning a new sixteen-story building, Newark's first "skyscraper").

Charles Cummings and I have particularly sought "story-telling" illustrations, the kind of paintings or photographs that are so intriguing in their own right that they almost can stand without captions. A few examples would be the 1845 fire in Newark, the four children of noted Civil War leader, Marcus L. Ward, the awesome jumble of horse-drawn streetcars and wagons in 1890 Newark, young men stepping off eagerly toward war, and the determined faces in both the Bethany Baptist Church choir of 1923 and the singers in today's Newark Boys Chorus.

Everything is history, even today's familiar items. A century from now, the ultra-modern architecture of buildings in Newark's Gateway project likely will seem quaint, or perhaps garish, to our descendants. Our proud clothes will be laugh-provoking costumes. Our modes of travel may then be as outmoded as yoked oxen. Our customs may seem bizarre.

Thus, for a sense of wonder, we can only remember. Our title stems from a suggestion by John O'Connor, respected friend, capable scholar, and fine teacher, who once felt he would do a book like this. We dedicate this work to him.

Selection of illustrations and sifting through them to choose about 275 of the best takes skill, knowledge, a feel for "picture telling" materials, and a knowledge of the surges of history. We especially appreciate the time and effort exerted for us by Howard W. Wiseman, long known for his uncanny ability to find the right illustration.

Charles Cummings and I appreciate that broad cross section of skilled Essex County historians, librarians, museum directors, and history buffs who aided us. We list them on page 189, urging them to realize they are far more to us in memory than a mere line of type might indicate.

Among those who have helped us in finding appropriate illustrations, we single out New Jersey Newsphotos, whose photographers each day enliven the pages of *The Star-Ledger*, New Jersey's largest and most widely read newspaper. They capture accurately and artistically modern history as it unfolds.

Most certainly we appreciate the encouragement lent us by Broad National Bancorporation and its chairman, Donald M. Karp.

JOHN T. CUNNINGHAM
FLORHAM PARK, NEW JERSEY
SUMMER 1995

Much of Essex County's geographical, historical, and spectacular essence comes clearly alive at Eagle Rock in West Orange, a major nineteenth century tourist attraction and still probably New Jersey's finest lookout. By day, the valley to the east teems with commerce; when darkness falls, it is brilliant to the far horizon with the glow from hundreds of thousands of homes and businesses.

Beyond, about fourteen miles away, are the towers of Manhattan. About midway in the panorama, slightly to the southeast, the tall buildings of downtown Newark loom. Immediately below Eagle Rock are the rooftops and tree crests of Montclair, Glen Ridge, and "the Oranges" (East, South, West) and the mother town, Orange itself.

Eagle Rock rises 630 feet above sea level, not high if compared to the Rockies, but then sea level here is only a dozen miles away. The lookout rests atop the highest of the two ridges of the Watchung Mountains, running north-south, and known locally as First and Second Mountain or "The Orange Mountains." These were barriers to early settlement and still divide the county almost in two.

The Watchung ridges are volcanic rock, formed 125 million

Artists of the nineteenth century found Eagle Rock a wildly romantic spot, as depicted in this first-known illustration of the famed Essex County area. It was sketched by Harry Fenn, noted Montclair artist, for his Picturesque America, *said to be the nation's first major "picture book" and predecessor to popular engravings in national illustrated newspapers. Courtesy the Newark Public Library.*

or so years ago when lava spewed from an ancient volcano, flowed underground through soft sandstone, and eventually was revealed when violent forces eroded the sandstone over hundreds of thousands of years. Nineteenth-century quarrying blasted huge chunks from the face of the cliff.

The second ridge of the Watchung Mountains (also known as the Orange Mountains) was hard basaltic rock cooled from the red-hot lava spewed forth by an ancient (and vanished) volcano of about one hundred million years ago. This was O'Rourke's quarry in Orange Township as it appeared in 1885. Courtesy the Newark Public Library.

Second Mountain is a divider in another way, for atop the ridges are two sprawling reservations, created in 1895 as part of the nation's first county park system under the aegis of the newly appointed Essex County Park Commission.

In 1895, a far-sighted *Newark Sunday Call* editor viewed the reservations as "the lungs of Essex County." In those days, when much of the county was still rural, reserving open lands seemed quixotic as well as unnecessary. Today the "lungs" make Essex far more than merely one huge city from county border to county border.

When Carl August Sommer painted this vision of Essex County's "mountain country" in the late nineteenth century, only a few evidences of habitation caught his artist's eye. The view from almost any vantage point in the Orange Mountains was (and still is) spectacular. Courtesy the Newark Museum.

Curiously, Essex is flanked on both east and west by the same stream, the Passaic River, making its slow, twisting journey from the interior of New Jersey to the sea. On the western border, the Passaic flows north; on the eastern, the flow is south.

This river brought the first colonists in May 1666. Through all the years since it has been a provider of power, a thoroughfare, and, until pollution fouled the water, a major source of drinking water and a prime recreation area.

(Left) Streams tumbling from the county's mountains, typified by Hemlock Falls in the South Mountain Reservation, provided the water power that early settlers needed for their mills. The purity of the mountain waters also appealed to hatters, tanners, and papermakers in Orange, Newark, and Millburn. Today, Hemlock Falls is merely scenic. Courtesy the Newark Public Library.

(Above) The Passaic River bounds both the eastern and western edges of Essex County and in May 1666 (as imagined by an 1877 artist), it brought the first settlers to the landing at a place they would call Newark. There the city—and Essex County—began. Courtesy the Newark Public Library.

(Above) The Newark Meadows of old contrasted sharply with the Orange Mountains, seen dimly in the background of this Meadows view painted in 1877 by Martin J. Heade. The area was used from earliest days as a place for grazing cattle and reaping hay. It is now almost completely covered by industrial plants and housing. Courtesy the Newark Museum.

CHAPTER I

WESTWARD
FROM THE RIVER

*Painted about seventy-five
years ago, this fanciful
depiction of the purchase of the
present site of Newark has some
probable inaccuracies (e.g. the
"Mohawk cut" on the Indian)
but it captures the spirit of the
exchange of an assortment of
lead bars, axes, coats, pistols,
swords, kettles, knives,
wampum, etc., for the land.
Courtesy Robert Treat
Conference Center.*

Several small boats worked slowly up the Passaic River
in mid-May of 1666, weighed down by thirty families,
household goods, livestock, fruit trees, and weapons.
These were fundamentalist Puritans from Connecticut, hopeful
that they had at last found their Zion, where church and government would be one forever.

No written record of the arrival survives, but tradition sets
the date as May 18. Assuming each family had an average of at
least six children, usual in those days, about 250 people landed
that day to found Newark and, eventually, Essex County.

Robert Treat, their leader, negotiated with Lenape Indians to
purchase title to the land. He secured a property that (using
modern place names) stretched from Newark Bay to the foot of

the Watchung Mountains, east to west; and from Clifton to Hillside, north to south. The settlers paid for the huge acreage with what now seems merely a curious miscellany:

Fifty double hands of powder, one hundred bars of lead, twenty axes, twenty coats, ten guns, twenty pistols, ten kettles, ten swords, four blankets, four barrels of beer, ten pair of breeches, fifty knives, twenty hoes, two ankers of liquor [about twenty gallons] or something equivalent, and three trooper's coats.

The Puritans named their settlement Newark, honoring the English home of their minister, the Reverend Abraham Pierson. They laid out a compact town centered on Broad and Market Streets, each 132 feet wide, the broadest street in colonial America. Plots were set aside for a market, militia training ground, cemetery, and church. Townspeople received six-acre tracts each, with Treat getting an extra two acres.

(That plan exists today in still-wide Broad and Market Streets; and in the marketplace, now Washington Park, and the militia ground, now Military Park, both on Broad Street.)

Determined to make Newark a theocracy with government centered in the meeting house, town fathers decreed that "to preserve the purity of religion," only those "as are members of some or other of the Congregational Churches" could dwell in the town. Eventually "outsiders" who could provide needed skills were permitted to become townspeople.

The town limits were increased to about sixty square miles on March 18, 1678, by extending the property to the top of the Orange Mountains. That tract, purchased from the Indians, included much of present-day Montclair, Glen Ridge, parts of the Oranges, and some of Millburn. The Indians received "two guns, three coats, and thirteen cans of rum."

Second-generation Newarkers began moving toward the

Early Newark's strong links to New England were evident in the first homes, such as this saltbox house built by Robert Treat in the center of town. He lived here only six years before returning to Connecticut, where he eventually became deputy governor, then governor, of the colony. Courtesy the Newark Public Library.

Robert Treat's statue stands atop the Settlers Monument in Newark's Fairmount Cemetery. Governor Treat's Newark home once stood at Broad and Market Streets, but disappeared long ago. Courtesy the Newark Public Library.

slopes after 1681, when the Newark Town Meeting surveyed highways "as far as the mountain." Cattle could be grazed there for milk, meat, and the hides that were coveted for tanning. Swiftly running streams provided power for gristmills and sawmills.

Those who moved to the northwest found that Dutch settlers had beaten them to the fertile soil in what is now Montclair's Brookdale section. The Dutch, too, had been wandering—from Bergen to Second River (now Belleville), and, following the Passaic River, to the upper portion of Essex County.

The Dutch sought permanency. Their Belleville kin had built houses from blocks of sandstone cut in a nearby quarry. The oldest structure was the Van Gieson house, built in 1691 and long known as "the Old Stone House of the Plains."

Two years after the Newarkers had moved close to the Dutch the New Jersey provincial legislature in 1683 designated four East Jersey counties—Essex, Monmouth, Middlesex, and Bergen. Essex sprawled across an area five or six times as large as the modern county.

The new Essex reached northward from Rahway to the border with New York, following the Hackensack River. The New York border, westward from the Hackensacks, was the county's northern edge for about twenty-seven miles. The Pequannock, Passaic, and Rahway Rivers formed the western borders and the southern boundary ran from about eight miles due west of Somerville to Rahway.

The map on page 19 shows those boundaries, as well as the three huge townships—Elizabethtown, Newark, and one called Acquickanick and New Barbadoes. This original Essex included all of modern Essex, Union, and Passaic Counties, and most of today's Bergen and Somerset Counties.

As the county expanded, Newark spawned small outlying settlements within Newark Township. Settlers who moved to the Orange Mountains and beyond, weary of the long treks to attend

A re-creation of one of the early homes of Old First Church. From this building the early community political and religious life was regulated. Courtesy the Newark Public Library.

At the General Assembly begun and holden at Elizabeth Towne in the Province of East New Jersey the first day of the Month Called March Anno Dom 1682. And in the four & thirteenth year of the Reign of King Charles the Second over England &c. and there Continued by Several Adjourned thereof untill the 28th day of the said Month of March for the Publick weake of this Province was Enacted as followeth

Having taken into Serious Consideration the Necessity of Dividing the Province into respective Countyes for the better governing and settling Courts in the Same Bee it Enacted by this General Assembly and the authority thereof that this Province be divided into foure Counties as followeth

Essex and the County thereof to Contain all the Settlements between the West Side of Hackinsack River & The parting Line between Woodbridge and Elizabeth Town & to Extend Westward and Northward to the Utmost bounds of the Province

Bergen County to Contain all the Settlements between Hudsons River & Hackensack River beginning at Constables hook and So to Extend to the Upper most bound of the Province Northward between the said Rivers

church services in the old town, established their own "meetings" or services in rustic little buildings or in their own homes. Tiny seeds of separation had been planted; it would take more than a century for full secession. Meanwhile, Newark Township encompassed all of the towns until 1806.

As the ex-Newarkers moved outward, crossroad hamlets were named for their leaders—Speertown (Upper Montclair), Cranetown (Montclair), Wardesson (Bloomfield), Squiertown (Livingston), Doddtown (East Orange), Camptown (Irvington), and Williamstown and Freemantown (both West Orange). A few places took names from local landmarks. In the west, a group of former Newarkers named their area "Horseneck," likely because of the river bend that seemed to resemble the shape of a horse's head. A roadside settlement called Cheapside (after the English "chepe," meaning "place where flocks are kept") eventually became part of Livingston.

Four counties were created by the General Assembly in Elizabethtown in 1682 for "the better governing" of the Province of East New Jersey. Thus was born Essex County along with Bergen, Monmouth, and Middlesex. Courtesy the Newark Public Library.

Place names were bestowed casually. James Camp, who moved southwest to the Elizabeth River, was honored by "Camp's Farms," then Camptown (decades later, Irvington). Nearby were "Great Wolf Harbour Swamp" and "Little Wolf Harbour Swamp," "Brushy Plain," and "Flaggy Swamp," the latter for the prolific summertime growth of wild flag lilies.

Camptown boasted of a colonial harbor with numerous docks. Small vessels, particularly sloops and periaugers, sailed into the harbor to exchange goods for local farm and woodland products.

The outward settlements were peopled with second and third generations of those who had come in 1666. They were the younger Cranes, Harrisons, Bruens, Baldwins, Wards, Dodds, Lindsleys, Swains, and others—names still familiar throughout the county.

Typical of restless young Newarkers was Azariah Crane, the eldest of Azariah Crane's many sons. He left the security of prosperous little Newark in 1694, trudged through the wilderness to "the great mountain called Watchung," and founded Cranetown. Dutch from Bergen County already had settled just to the north in what they called Speertown. It took seventy-four years—until 1768—to build a road connecting the neighboring (but not neighborly) villages.

"The Mountain Society" was organized to build a church atop Orange Mountain. The local farmers planted apple orchards, producing cider and some no-

The original bounds of Essex County, drawn in 1682, included an area more than four times as large as modern Essex. The county had three townships—Elizabethtown, Newark, and one named Acquickanick and New Barbadoes. This large, ungovernable county persisted until 1709, when the northern area was allotted to Bergen County and much of the southwestern portion was given to Somerset County. Elizabethtown Township remained part of Essex until 1857. Map from John P. Snyder's The Story of New Jersey's Civil Boundaries, 1606–1968.

table applejack. After 1723, when a productive copper mine was opened on John Dodd's farm, prospectors roamed the mountain.

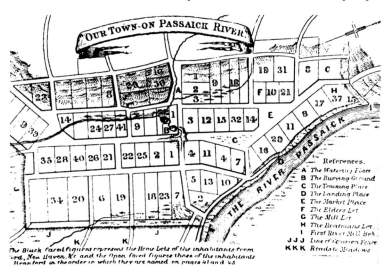

"Our Town on Passaick River," as laid out in 1668, centered on Broad and Market Streets, then occupied by a spring that fed two nearby ponds. The "Watering Place," for livestock initially, soon became the gathering place for colonial tanners. Note the low bluff along the river and the area H (lots 37 and 15), set aside for the town's official boatmen. Courtesy the Newark Public Library.

A nineteenth century artist's interpretation of Newark's first shocking episode, when Colonel Josiah Ogden and family, Presbyterians all, cut wheat on a Sunday, breaking the Sabbath. Tradition says the action led to founding Trinity Episcopal Church in 1746. Atkinson, History of Newark, New Jersey.

All of them, farmers, cider makers, and prospectors, united around the first church established outside of Newark—a radical break with the home town.

Religious differences split the town of Newark in 1733. Newark's church had evolved into Presbyterian leadership, maintaining the rigid Puritan beliefs. Close by, across the river in Bergen County and in nearby Elizabethtown, many settlers followed Church of England doctrines. Elizabethtown, still part of Essex County and a rival for county leadership, installed its first Church of England pastor in 1708.

The schism in Newark was led by a leading Presbyterian and staunch Newarker, Colonel Josiah Ogden. In the late summer of 1733, Ogden's wheat lay cut in the fields during a rainy spell. The sun came out on a Sunday morning and dried the wheat. Ogden and his family harvested the crop—on the Lord's Day.

Ogden was tried for violating Sunday strictures, found guilty, and rebuked so severely that he left the church. He and other dissidents founded a new congregation based on Episcopal theology. They met in private homes for many years, then chartered Trinity Church in 1746. On a half-acre tract at the north end of Military Park they built the high-steepled church that still stands on its original site.

Disturbed by the split, the Newark Presbyterians reached out to Morris County to invite youthful Aaron Burr to become their minister. The boyish pastor,

This print was drawn shortly after Episcopalians finished Trinity Episcopal Church in 1746. The substantial building towered over the few small houses along Broad Street, then little more than a dirt road. This is likely the oldest contemporary view of Newark. Courtesy the Newark Museum.

intelligent and impassioned, became the spiritual leader on January 25, 1737, twenty-one days after his twenty-first birthday.

Burr's brilliant leadership revived the church and made him the natural choice in 1747 to succeed the Reverend Jonathan Dickinson of Elizabethtown, as president of the College of New Jersey. Dickinson died in the early autumn of 1747, a year after he had founded the college, the first in New Jersey, in October 1746. Upon Dickinson's death, the eight students agreed to study under Burr's tutelage.

The college remained in Newark for nine years, turning out mostly Presbyterian ministers. Its most noted graduate was Richard Stockton, a lawyer and, later, a signer of the Declaration of Independence. Stockton was a leading influence in relocating the College of New Jersey in 1756 from Newark to an imposing stone building in Princeton. There it began its rise toward its eventual eminent status as Princeton University.

Burr's tenure at Princeton lasted only a year; he died there in 1757 at age forty-one. Perhaps more significant nationally was his marriage in Newark on June 29, 1752, to Esther Edwards of Massachusetts, the third daughter of Jonathan Edwards, noted fire-and-brimstone preacher. Their son, Aaron Jr., born in 1756 at the Newark parsonage, became one of the most intriguing and most controversial figures in American history. He became vice president of the United States, under Thomas Jefferson.

Trouble that had far-reaching effects stirred the entire county of Essex in mid-September, 1745. Proprietors arrested Samuel Baldwin, charged him with illegally cutting wood in the Horseneck, and hauled him off to the crude little Essex County jail in Newark to await trial.

First Presbyterian Church in Orange is an outgrowth of the first simple wooden structure built after Nathaniel Wheeler, one of the founders of Newark, laid out the burying ground and established the Mountain Society in 1765. Courtesy the Newark Public Library.

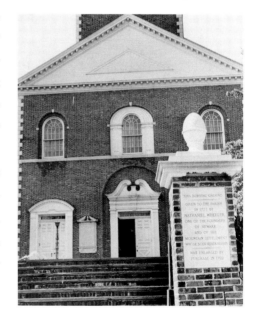

About 150 enraged Horseneckers stormed into town on Sunday, September 19, defied the sheriff, and burst open the jail, freeing Baldwin. They warned that the next time they would be back "with double the number of men." Despite the threat, the sheriff arrested three more men in the Horseneck on January 15, 1746, and jailed them in Newark.

A howling mob promptly freed the prisoners, despite a "King's Proclamation . . . against riots." The rebellious spirit spread through New Jersey until Governor Lewis Morris warned that such "contempt of the laws came close to high treason, . . . likely to end in rebellion and throwing off his Majesty's authority."

The outbreak of the French and Indian War solidified the colonists and ended the riots, but a torch had been lit. Except for the Crown-devoted Episcopalians, most of Essex County leaned toward opposition to what they considered England's "acts of tyranny"—the Stamp Act, the Sugar Act, the Boston Massacre, and all the other incidents that led to the American Revolution.

Newark's Presbyterian strength survived the bitter aftermath

of Colonel Ogden's wheat gathering in 1733; the town was overwhelmingly anti-British as the American Revolution approached. Those who lived in the Horseneck had been the first to rebel. Elsewhere in the sparsely settled hinterlands, few supporters of King George could be found.

Hostility exploded into the open in November 1774, when Chief Justice Frederick Smythe, appointed by the Crown, warned an Essex County grand jury that protesting colonists feared "imaginary tyranny" rather than looking for "real tyranny at our own doors."

Irate jurors told Smythe in a long, rancorous answer that taxes imposed by England, or "depriving us of the inestimable right of trial by jury" or "carrying us for trial to Great Britain," was not "tyranny merely imaginary."

War in its fullest fury came to Essex County only once. As Washington retreated across the state toward Pennsylvania in November 1776, Newarkers were advised to take livestock, grains, carriages, and all valuables westward to the mountains. On November 21, women and children left the town.

George Washington led his dispirited troops into Newark on November 22. That night, in a pouring rain, Thomas Paine sat by a smoking fire in one of the town parks and began to write his famous *Crisis Papers*. His call to valor began with the memorable "These are the times that try men's souls. . . ."

Inexplicably, the British tarried to the north for five days.

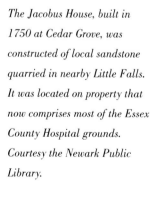

The Jacobus House, built in 1750 at Cedar Grove, was constructed of local sandstone quarried in nearby Little Falls. It was located on property that now comprises most of the Essex County Hospital grounds. Courtesy the Newark Public Library.

The Lane-Corey House, built sometime before 1765 in West Caldwell, is seen here in a twentieth century photograph that shows owner Josephine Mahon and her garden. Courtesy the Newark Evening News.

Finally, on November 28, the American army retreated out of Newark, headed for New Brunswick and on to the temporary encampment on the Pennsylvania side of the Delaware River. There, on Christmas Day, the Americans recrossed the river for rousing victories at Trenton and Princeton.

Hope revived in Essex County as well in the rest of the nation. Tories, who a month before had joyously welcomed the British to Newark, fled to New York. Among them was the Reverend Isaac Browne, rector of Trinity Church.

Except for raids, Essex County did not again know the full impact of war. Militiamen in the western part of the county manned the string of warning beacons on the Watchung Mountains, particularly "Washington Rock" in today's South Mountain Reservation. The beacons helped call militiamen from Essex and elsewhere for the critical Battle of Springfield on June 23, 1780.

The end of the war left Essex only slightly touched physically; burned-out Newark Academy was the only major loss. Far more hurtful was the departure of many Essex County Tories headed toward exile in Nova Scotia. Among them was one John

The Joseph Crane homestead in Montclair was built for Crane's bride, Hannah Lamson, who married Crane shortly before the onset of the Revolutionary War. Courtesy the Newark Evening News.

Edison. Nearly ninety years later, his grandson, Thomas Alva Edison, would return to Essex County.

In the aftermath of the war, county residents began to face their problems. Only the crudest of roads led in or out of Newark, the only well-populated town in the county. Outward to the mountains and beyond, even worse roads were all that linked that "outside world" with Newark. Essex County was, in fact, far off the beaten track.

The snug little John Speer House, built in Belleville in 1789, has a "Williamsburg look." The picket fence, heavy chimney, and shuttered windows add to the illusion of a colonial Virginia dwelling. Courtesy the Newark Evening News.

One of the most intriguing houses of early Newark was the Meeker Homestead in the Lyons Farm area of the city. The shingled building, while altered and expanded since it was erected in about 1676, appeared sound in this photograph taken in 1901, shortly before the 225-year-old farmhouse was demolished. Courtesy the Newark Public Library.

Newark's Sydenham House, one of the city's two oldest residences, was built circa 1712 by John and Susannah Sydenham along the Old Road to Bloomfield in the Forest Hill section, adjacent to Branch Brook Park. Courtesy D. J. and Elizabeth Henderson.

The Plume House on Broad Street, Newark, was erected in about 1725. When constructed, the structure was surrounded by open fields and orchards. Today it is next to the old Erie-Lackawanna Railroad station in a busy part of the city. Courtesy the Newark Public Library.

(Below) Belleville made considerable contributions to colonial New Jersey's industrial history and Archibald Robertson lent beauty to Bennett's Grist Mill in this handsome watercolor executed early in the nineteenth century. Courtesy the New Jersey Historical Society.

Reverend Aaron Burr Sr., minister of Old First Church from 1737 to 1755, nursed the struggling little College of New Jersey to health and took it off to Princeton in 1756. He is best known, however, because he fathered Aaron Burr Jr., the high-spirited political leader who fatally wounded Alexander Hamilton in a duel at Weehawken in 1804. Courtesy the Newark Public Library.

This Gilbert Stuart portrait of Aaron Burr Jr., future vice president of the United States, was found in a cabin in an isolated part of Millburn. It is now owned by the New Jersey Historical Society. Burr was born in Newark in 1856, the year the College of New Jersey moved from Newark to Princeton. Courtesy the New Jersey Historical Society.

Aaron Burr Sr. brought his bride to this parsonage on Broad Street in 1752, set on the site of Old First Church. She was Esther Edwards, daughter of the well-known, fiery preacher Jonathan Edwards of Massachusetts. Two children, Sally and Aaron Burr Jr. were born here. Courtesy the Newark Public Library.

This is the founding document for the College of New Jersey, established in Elizabethtown in 1746. After its founder died within a year, the college was transferred to Newark, where eight students studied under Mr. Burr in the courtroom above the county jail. Courtesy Princeton University.

(Right) The Timothy Ball House, now in Maplewood, built in 1743 by a cousin of George Washington, was an important site in Essex County Revolutionary War history. During the War, General Washington spent many hours in the house and is said to have slept in the small room over the kitchen. Courtesy the Newark Public Library.

Millburn's "Old Hessian House," which has been described as "one of the most striking examples of early American farmhouses," was started sometime before 1750. It is known as the Hessian House because two of the German mercenaries are believed to have hidden in the attic after the Battle of Springfield on June 23, 1780. Courtesy the Newark Public Library.

Francis D. Millett's mural in Essex County Court House depicts the foreman of the 1774 Grand Jury rebuking Chief Justice Frederick Smythe for his harsh judgment that Americans imagined "tyranny." The foreman sharply told Smythe that taxation and the blockading of Boston Harbor went far beyond imagination. Courtesy the Newark Public Library.

However stylized this rough woodcut from Atkinson's 1878 History of Newark *might be, it catches the spirit of November 22, 1776, when Washington led his dispirited troops into Newark for a brief pause before retreating southward to an eventual crossing of the Delaware River. Atkinson,* History of Newark, New Jersey.

The first home of the Newark Academy, built in 1774, served in the early years of the American Revolution as a temporary barracks and hospital during Washington's retreat through town in November 1776. British raiders torched the building in a raid in January 1780. Courtesy the Newark Public Library.

The Battle of Springfield on June 23, 1780, was Essex County's most important military operation in the War. Rev. James Caldwell, whose wife had been killed by a British sniper only two weeks before, gained lasting fame when he threw armloads of Watts' hymnals to use as wadding, shouting "Give 'em Watts!" Caldwell's virulent anti-British sentiments earned him the title "high priest of the Revolution." Courtesy Fraunces Tavern, New York City.

CHAPTER 2

GROWTH
AMID DIVISION

The Reverend Alexander Macwhorter, (above) pastor of Newark's Old First Church from 1759 until he died in 1807, was the rock on which Newark rebuilt after the Revolution. Called a "revolutionist, educator, and booster of Newark," he was a dominant force as the place stretched from a church-controlled colonial town to a bustling small town. A new "Old First," shown in a contemporary print (left) was the highlight of Pastor Macwhorter's forty-eight-year stay in Newark. It has served for more than two centuries. Courtesy the Newark Public Library.

When George Washington triumphantly crossed New Jersey in April 1789, on his way to his inauguration as President of the United States, he naturally stayed overnight in Elizabethtown. The next morning he left there by ferry for the trip across New York Bay. The thought of going into Newark, then venturing across the treacherous meadows to the Paulus Hook (now Jersey City) ferry never crossed his mind.

The dramatic turning point in early Essex County history came in 1790, when the State Legislature agreed that the "public good" would be enhanced by a sixty-four-foot-wide roadway from the Newark courthouse to Paulus Hook, featured by long wooden bridges over the wide Passaic and Hackensack Rivers.

The bridges were a monumental undertaking. The financial backers hired Josiah Nottage, the nation's finest bridge builder, who had just finished a span over the Charles River to join Boston and Cambridge. Nottage hired "twenty carpenters and a number of labourers." They finished both bridges in the summer of 1795: the Passaic span was 492 feet long and the Hackensack bridge, 930 feet.

Conquering the oozing marshes between the bridges required an ingenious road "made of logs laid across the road close together, of three or four layers, and covered with sod and earth dug up on each side; over this is laid gravel." Travelers willingly paid the Passaic River Bridge tolls: "four cents for man and horse; ten cents for horse and chair; twenty-nine cents for coach or light wagon with two horses; and thirty-nine cents for vehicles

Long before New Jersey had a system of free public education, Lyons Farm Schoolhouse was built in the south part of Newark in 1784. It was a school for more than a century. The building was moved to the Newark Museum garden in 1938 and restored. Courtesy the Newark Public Library.

David Alling opened his Newark "fancy chair" establishment in 1790 in the building on the right, which also served as his home. Later he built the small shop to the left. Alling's fame spread far beyond the city and state; in turn, he was host when such visiting Frenchmen as the Vicomte de Chateaubriand and the Duc de Talleyrand-Perigord visited Newark. Courtesy the Newark Museum.

with four horses." Tolls were a bit higher on the Hackensack span.

Cross-state travelers quickly opted for the new routes. Carriages rolled noisily through Newark streets, bringing newspapers, mail, and passengers willing to comment on the news of the outside world as they supped at Arch Gifford's Hounds and Horn tavern.

The emerging town reveled in holiday parades that featured marching craftsmen—tanners, shoemakers, cordwainers, wheelwrights, hatters, millers, clothiers, blacksmiths, and others. Some of the marchers were from outlying places, but not many; industry was just beginning in the western villages.

On the western slopes, trade began to stir in the place called "Rum Brook," named for the pleasant odor of the applejack mash that was dumped upstream. The village had other, less-colorful names: Riverhead, Vaux Hall, and Milltown. The fragrant brook flowed into the Rahway (locally called the Raw Way) River.

Samuel Campbell of New York built a mill on the sweet-smelling brook in 1790 to make a high-quality paper that bore the watermark of the thistle, symbol of Campbell's native home in Scotland. Campbell and other Scots much later influenced the choice of Millburn (Mill River) as the town name. Within a few years after Campbell's start, five town dams backed up five millponds to meet the water needs of papermakers.

A few of the papermakers also manufactured hats, believing minerals in the mountain spring water softened the furs used to make headwear. That theory also enticed James Condit to make

This "Boy's Lodging House and Children's Aid Society" might have been Moses Combs' greatest contribution to history, despite the fact that in 1790 Combs founded a shoemaking factory in Newark that sold products as far away as Georgia, establishing Newark's huge trade with the South. However, Combs valued educated apprentices. He built this home and school to house them and train them. Many "Combs boys" became major figures in Newark's broad-based leather industries. Courtesy the Newark Public Library.

Lotteries were much in academic and religious favor on July 3, 1793, when Newark Academy boosters sought funds to rebuild the academy burned by the British. Courtesy the Newark Public Library.

the first hats in Orange in 1785. But Cyrus Jones won credit for "pulling Orange prosperity out of a hat" when he turned a few beaver furs into hats in 1790.

Jones walked to New York, sold his hats, then bought furs to make more. He urged his apprentices to strike out on their own; within a few years, "all the running streams of the region were colored red" from the dyes dumped in streams by Orange's thirty-two hat factories.

The most prominent hat name in Orange was Stetson. The first of the famous family, Stephen, began in 1790. Four of his sons became Orange hatters, most notably John, maker and popularizer of the broad-brimmed "western" Stetson hat, the symbol of rawboned, sunbaked cowboys on the prairies.

Second River, founded by Dutch settlers about five miles north of Newark's center, began industrial resurgence after a bridge was finished in 1793 across the Passaic River to open the way toward New York. Four years before, a nearby copper mine had been reopened. The town had begun to reach for the copper-making prominence it would later earn.

Second River's early industrial fame stemmed from the Soho machine works opened by James Roosevelt in 1794. There he built his first homemade steam powered boat, working closely with John Stevens, the first to use steam extensively on the Hudson River; and Robert Fulton, who steamed the much-praised steamboat *Clermont* from New York to Albany in 1807. Proud of

Belleville's John and William Sanford launched their first steamboat on October 21, 1797, about ten years before Robert Fulton won overblown praise for his steamboat trip to Albany in 1807. This is the Proprietor, *one of several rear paddlewheel steamboats produced at Belleville. Courtesy the Newark Public Library.*

Improved colonial taverns and "modern" stagecoaches replaced outmoded forms of wayside inns and means of transportation early in the nineteenth century, when privately built turnpikes (toll roads) were built. Stagecoach routes ran to Camptown (Irvington), Bloomfield, Livingston, and elsewhere in the county. Courtesy the Newark Public Library.

their town's industrial accomplishments, Second River residents opted for a more elegant name in 1797, choosing Belleville ("beautiful town").

Travelers of the time heaped accolades on Newark. In 1793, Henry Wansey of England climbed up nearly two hundred feet in the steeple of First Church, then only three years old. Newark, in his mind, was "peculiarly elegant." A year later, another Englishman, Thomas Twining, called Newark "one of the neatest and prettiest towns I have ever seen."

The Duke de la Rochefault of France, was more perceptive than either Wansey or Twining (although he did call Newark "one of the finest villages in America"). The Duke wrote of a shoemaker "who manufactures shoes for exportation" and employed "between three hundred and four hundred workmen."

That shoemaker was Moses Combs, a clergyman without a pulpit, who began making shoes in town in 1790. Combs had piercing black eyes, the outward manifestation of his zeal, whether sewing uppers or saving souls. In his first year as a shoemaker, Combs shipped two hundred pairs of sealskin shoes to Savannah, Georgia. With that sale, Combs began the huge trade with the South that eventually shaped Newark's strong support for the South when the Civil War impended.

Artist's depiction of Christmas morning in 1804 at the handsome Fairfield Dutch Reformed Church, set in the center of widespread, snow-covered fields. Courtesy the Newark Public Library.

Combs built a combination church and school for his young workers, said to be the first apprentice school in America. Many laborers who learned to read and write in the school became trade leaders as Newark emerged as a prime center of all kinds of leather manufacture and use.

Despite the bridges, Moses Combs, the Orange hatters, and the Millburn papermakers, Essex County remained sparsely populated outside of Newark. Cattle and sheep drovers from Sussex County and beyond still rested their herds in Cheapside (part of Livingston), waiting for peak prices in Newark and New York. Slow-moving haywagons and drays, heavily laden with hinterland vegetables, cheese, and applejack, rolled through the mountain passes, vying for room with the drovers.

Census takers in 1800 reported the surprising news that the supposed wilderness of far-off Sussex County had more people than Essex. True, Sussex encompassed what would become Warren County; but on the other hand, Essex still contained all of Union County.

Good sense, plus a hope for profits, prompted Essex industrialists to pin their hopes on swiftly changing modes of transportation, starting with the privately run, toll-charging turnpike craze that swept across New Jersey in the first third of the nineteenth century. One toll road ran from Newark to Springfield to join the turnpike that went to Morristown and Phillipsburg. Another ran westward through Livingston (today's Mt. Pleasant Avenue). The county's pride was the Newark-Pompton Turnpike, from Newark to Cranesville (later Montclair), then on to Pompton.

Israel ("King") Crane staked

Israel Crane, a descendant of both Robert Treat and Jasper Crane, two of Newark's founders, was one of the major developers of western Essex County in the formative years. He built this home in 1796 on the Old Road in Cranetown (now Montclair) and became the prime merchant for a wide area. Crane enhanced his fortune and reputation in 1807 when he became the major force in constructing the Newark-Pompton Turnpike (now Bloomfield Avenue). The Crane home was moved in 1965 from its original site to Orange Road, a mile and a half away, where it is a museum house. Courtesy Montclair Historical Society.

his reputation and some of his fortune on that turnpike to Craneville in the western part of Bloomfield Township. Directly descended from Newark's founders, Crane owned a wide-traveling fleet of wagons that brought him power and wealth.

Newark had a scare in 1807, when Elizabeth (the colonial "town" suffix had been dropped) sought voter approval to have a proposed new Essex County courthouse set in their town. The long distance to polling places necessitated three days of voting—in Day's Hill (now part of Irvington) the first day, Elizabeth the second, and Newark the third.

William Pennington

Elizabeth had a strong lead after the first two days. Thoroughly aroused and alerted, Newarkers set out to overcome the known handicap. Polls opened at 1 A.M. (five or six hours earlier than usual) on the third day and continued until sundown—a sixteen-hour voting day, a dream for politicians bent on chicanery.

Women then could vote in New Jersey. They did, on that third day:

After the 1812 State Legislature authorized state banks, Newarkers organized the National State Bank and erected this structure in 1813, the same year that William Pennington, National's first president, also became governor of New Jersey.

The Harrison House, a typical farmhouse in Roseland, was built in 1824 in the empire classical style. It is now the home of the Roseland Historical Society. Courtesy Roseland Historical Society.

as themselves, in men's clothing, in blackface, and in other disguises, acting as men commonly did on election day. When the sun set, Newark counted more votes than it had residents. The old Puritan town easily won the courthouse, 7,666 to 6,181, even as it lost some of its virtue.

Properly pious state legislators knew what to do: They barred all New Jersey women from voting, and for good measure added all Indians, foreigners, blacks, and idiots. Blacks (men only) got the vote back in 1875. Women had to wait until 1920.

By 1807 the breakup of old Newark Township had begun. Caldwell Township split away in 1798, taking most of western Essex. Orange followed in 1806, in a township that included all of today's Oranges and Maplewood. Two other major se-

"Broad and Market" has been the heart of Essex County's principal town (and city) since 1667. Looking southeast from the intersection sometime between 1812 and 1820, an unknown artist saw little beyond the streetfront buildings except the old burying ground and open fields. In the foreground, the town pump is in the center and to the left is the sign of Archer Gifford's widely known tavern and stagecoach stop. Courtesy the Newark Museum.

cessions soon followed. The first became Bloomfield, named for New Jersey's fourth governor, Joseph Bloomfield; the large area included today's Bloomfield, Belleville, Verona, Glen Ridge, and Montclair. The second, formed in 1813, became Livingston, named for New Jersey's first governor.

Growth was slow for the next two decades. In 1832 and 1833, when the noted geographer and gazetteer Thomas Gordon made his enduring survey of New Jersey, he reported Essex inhabitants "have the love of order, decorum, industry, and thrift of their ancestors."

More to the point, he reported on specific industry. Over and above the expected gristmills and sawmills, he found in the county: "22 cotton and 13 woolen manufactories, 19 paper mills, 223 vats for tanning leather, 3 bleaching and printing establishments for cotton, and 5 distilleries." Surprisingly, he did not mention hatters in his summary, but in a report on Orange he told of "a large trade . . . in the manufacture of leather, shoes and hats." Gordon found Belleville thriving from a concentration of copper and brass processing factories.

Peter Maverick, Newark's famous engraver, was thirty-eight years old when portraitist John Neagle painted him in 1826. He opened an engraving shop in the town in 1802 and soon after hired Asher B. Durand of Jefferson Village (now Maplewood). Both achieved fame, Maverick as an engraver, Durand as a painter) and in 1826 they founded the National Academy of Design. Courtesy the Newark Public Library.

Newark had three banks as the 1830s began. The first, Newark Banking and Insurance Company, dated to 1804. Gordon wrote of the huge increase in property values and described Newark in terms of "noble trees," "wholesome water," and "costly, elegant and commodious homes."

Gordon had an eye for hard facts: "the facilities for communication with New York render the town [Newark] a suburb of the great city." It was no exaggeration. More than sixty-five vessels made Newark a port of call, including two ships that sailed the world in search of whales. Romantic though that seemed, far more important to Essex County was the Morris Canal—finished from Phillipsburg to Newark in 1831—and the Morris & Essex Railroad, chartered the same year to link Newark and Morristown. The money-strapped railroad finally reached Morristown in 1838 and Dover in 1845.

The railroad gave Seth Boyden, Newark's inventive genius, the attention he had long deserved. Railroad financiers despaired of finding a locomotive able to conquer the mountains to the west. They turned to Boyden, a modest man who had perfected in Newark America's first patent leather and the first malleable iron. He preferred anonymity to wealth and fame. Boyden built the locomotive and was at the throttle on the day it rose over the heights to Summit, the last obstacle to points west.

The railroad, canal, and port so enhanced the many and varied industrial plants that in 1836 town fathers shed the colonial "town" designation to receive a state charter as a city. The city government rented space in the county courthouse that had been won in the election of 1807. When the structure burned down

Earliest view of today's Ironbound (East Ward) section of Newark. In the background is the "S" curve of the Passaic River and two small ships sailing on Newark Bay. The time was about 1830, when housing had spread eastward along Market Street to far parts of the marshlands. On this very site Newark was founded in 1666. Today it is the site of the Gateway Center and now under construction is the future home of the New Jersey Performing Arts Center at Newark. Here Newark was founded and is being reborn. Courtesy the Newark Public Library.

in 1837, the city and county resumed the relationship in a new courthouse built a year later.

Harmony gave way to discord outside the city. Old Essex County was about to break apart. Hostility toward Newark by "Elizabethans" exceeded anything that could be imagined. They had been angry almost from Newark's founding, believing the Puritans had unfairly lured away Elizabeth's colonial leather prominence. But nothing stung more than the ill-fated courthouse election of 1807. Elizabeth people wanted a divorce—and won it in 1857 to become New Jersey's twenty-first and last county. Interestingly, as the nation itself edged toward secession, the people in the new county ignored the fact of their own secession and named their county Union.

It didn't matter much to Essex. Nearly all of the industrial, financial, transportation, and political power remained in Newark and its sister towns. Disunion proved to be highly beneficial for Essex: the county finally had become manageable.

The Old Brick Store, built in about 1800 in West Caldwell, housed the town council's first meeting and later was the community's firehouse. Courtesy the Newark Public Library.

William Hardenberg delineated
Newark's Trinity Church in
watercolors in about 1825.
He also included the muddy ruts
of Broad Street and the fenced-
in militia green. Courtesy
the Newark Public Library.

Brick Church, built in 1831 at
the corner of Prospect and Main
Streets in East Orange, gave its
name to the surrounding section
and to the Brick Church stop on
the D.L. & W. Railroad. Courtesy
the Newark Museum.

Few New Jerseyans deserve the limelight more than Newark's Seth Boyden and few get as little as he. A native New Englander, he came to Newark in 1815, and perfected such things as America's first patent leather (1821) and the nation's first malleable iron (1826). He turned his attention to railroads in 1835 and invented the nation's first locomotive capable of pulling loads up steep hills. The Morris & Essex Railroad used Boyden's engines to conquer steep First and Second Mountains. The mural shows a Boyden engine idling in Maplewood while the inventor talked to a fascinated little boy.

Courtesy the Newark Public Library

Courtesy the Newark Public Library

The old Essex County Jail, built in 1837 from plans drawn by famed architect, John Haviland, was near the Morris Canal. Looking more like a country estate than a jail, the structure is now a historic landmark. Courtesy the Newark Public Library.

Orange's first public school, built in 1848, served until 1882 when it became a private dwelling. Later it was part of a lumber plant. Courtesy the Newark Public Library.

An artist sat east of the Passaic
River in about 1840 to paint this
portrait of Belleville, fronting
on the busy river and clustered
within the lengthened shadows
of the high-steepled Dutch
Reformed Church. Painting
owned in 1948 by Mrs. Henry W.
Goodrich of Nutley, New Jersey.

Newark's great fire of 1845 swept
along Broad Street opposite
Trinity Church. It exposed,
as did all fires in all towns,
the hopelessness of firemen trying
to stem flames with pitifully
inadequate equipment and
no dependable water supply.
Courtesy the Newark Museum.

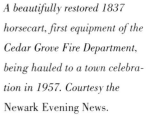

A beautifully restored 1837 horsecart, first equipment of the Cedar Grove Fire Department, being hauled to a town celebration in 1957. Courtesy the Newark Evening News.

Known originally as "The Old Manse," the home for Caldwell Presbyterian Church ministers, this house became the birthplace of Grover Cleveland in 1837— but did not become important until he was elected president of the United States in 1884 (and again in 1892 after losing in 1888). It became a historic site in 1913, administered by the Cleveland Birthplace Memorial Association. WPA workers restored the building during the Depression of the 1930s. It is now a state-run Historic Site. Courtesy New Jersey Newsphotos.

John W. Barber and Henry Howe's remarkable Historical Collections of New Jersey *included Bloomfield's "substantial stone" Presbyterian Church and village green; "an eastern view of Bellville" that contrasted sharply with the pristine watercolor on page 47; Newark's very wide, very built-up Broad street; and the "new" $71,000 Egyptian-style courthouse, finished in 1838 to replace the earlier courthouse destroyed by fire in August 1835. Barber and Howe,* Historical Collections of New Jersey.

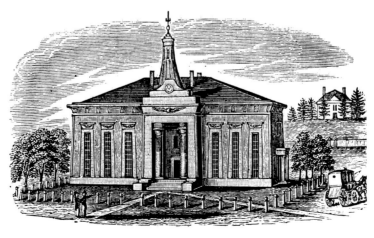

Professor James J. Mapes, pioneer in soil fertilization, bought a run-down farm in Clinton Township in 1847 and revived it with generous applications of bone meal and super phosphate of lime. He became known as the state's and nation's "pioneer scientific agriculturist." Shaw, History of Essex and Hudson Counties.

The Morris Canal brought prosperity to Bloomfield, Belleville, and Newark in the 1830s. A myriad of canalboats, such as that shown here tied up awaiting a cargo from L. M. Smith leatherworks, plied the canal. Beyond freight, the canal offered pleasure rides (twenty-five cents, Newark to Bloomfield; fifty cents, Newark to Paterson). The "people's dividend" was winter skating, particularly near Belleville's Soho section. Courtesy the Newark Public Library.

LIVERY STABLES.

MATTHIAS CLINTOCK,
Livery and Exchange Stable, 9 William-street, n. Broad.

WILLIAM COMPTON,
Livery Stable, 160 Market-street, near Broad.

JESSE R. DONALDSON,
Livery and Exchange Stable, 398 Broad c. Hill-street.

ANDREW TEED,
Livery Stable, 162 Washington-street, near Market.

STEPHEN BOND,
Livery Stable, 60 Halsey-street, near the Church.

H. A. MOURISON,
Livery Stable, 127 Washington, corner of Academy-street.

JOHN C. MOORE,
Livery Stable, 318 Broad-street, U. S. Hotel.

ASA THOMAS,
Livery Stable, 251 Market-street corner Alling.

WILLIAM STARRS,
Livery Stable, 188 Broad, near New-street.

WILLIAM W. MONROE,
Livery Stable, corner South Market and Ferry-street.

CHARLES BROWN,
Livery Stable, 1 Harrison-street, near Market.

JACOB YOUNGBLOOD,
Livery Stable, 124 Broad-street.

Livery stables were to the nineteenth century what gas stations are to the automobile age. The Newark City Directory for 1842 listed twelve stables within hailing distance of the city's center. Courtesy the Newark Public Library.

David Oakes' cassimere (variation of cashmere) works, opened in Bloomfield in about 1830, as it appeared in 1850. Oakes' home on Belleville Avenue is now a cultural center and museum, called "Oakeside." Courtesy the Newark Evening News.

Michael Nerney, whaler, captain of a ship in trade with South America, and a New Jersey pilot charged with bringing ships into Newark, long argued for lighthouses at Newark Bay and Bergen Point. Congress heeded his plea in 1847, allocated $18,000 for the two lights, and appointed Nerney as first keeper of the Newark Bay lighthouse shown here. It remained operative until 1914. Courtesy the Newark Evening News.

This portion of Newark appeared in an 1850 picture book, showing several imposing factories and other buildings. It also showed considerable substandard housing, the forerunner of city slums. Courtesy the Newark Public Library.

(Above) Fairfield's "Country Corner Store," now a tourist attraction, was opened in 1855 to serve the surrounding agricultural area. Courtesy the Newark Evening News.

(Left) Episcopalians bought the old Plume farm in northern Newark in 1850 and finished their high-steepled Gothic church by 1856, the year this etching appeared. The church became known as the "House of Prayer." Courtesy the Newark Public Library.

(Below) Essex County's hosting of the New Jersey Agricultural State Fair in 1856 was featured in Frank Leslie's Illustrated Newspaper on September 27, 1856. Initially staged on a large field in northeastern Newark, close to Belleville, the fair shifted to Waverly, now Weequahic Park, in 1867 and continued there until the 1890s. Frank Leslie's Illustrated Newspaper, 1856.

Except for the white servant holding the horse, this might have been a Georgia family posed on the steps of a southern mansion on the eve of the Civil War. Instead, it was the John F. Ogden family lined up for a portrait at their High Street home in Newark. Courtesy the Newark Museum.

CHAPTER 3

THE PACE OF WAR— AND PEACE

Everything moved too fast for most Essex County people as the 1850s wore down. Taxpayers grumbled about the cost of such niceties as gaslights to brighten streets, wooden walks to keep women's skirts out of the mud, watchmen "by day and by night" to keep the peace, and better schools to prepare children for a rapidly changing world. Soon such disagreement would fragment the county.

When Union County seceded in 1857, Essex was largely rural except for Newark, the industrial sections of Orange and Belleville, and emerging centers in Montclair and Bloomfield. The 1860 Census reported nearly seventy-five percent of the county was farmland; the Essex County Agricultural Society, founded in Orange in 1821, had long been noted for its annual fair and farm show.

Increasing numbers of Irish and German immigrants in the 1840s and 1850s headed for Newark, where the wide variety of industries, from beer to shoes, carriages to clothing, varnish to jewelry, needed skills and muscles. Only Orange's hat and shoe factories, Belleville's copper-working plants, and Bloomfield's modest woolen factory offered even slight competition to Newark.

The future pace of Essex had been set by the Morris Canal, the Morris & Essex Railroad, and the docks on the Passaic River at Newark and Belleville. Business leaders in Newark and New York followed the railroad tracks outward to the Oranges and Millburn. After 1856, the Newark & Bloomfield Railroad branched off from the M. & E. at Roseville in Newark, offering the benefits of commuting as far as West Bloomfield, soon to become Montclair.

By the late 1850s, the smoldering national hatred between North and South was on everyone's mind. That came intimately home on February 1, 1860, when William Pennington of Newark was elected Speaker of the House of Representatives to end fifty-nine days of rancorous sectional debate that had completely stalled national legislation.

Pro-southern sentiment prevailed in Newark and Orange, where manufacturers sought to protect their huge markets in the South. Edward M. Fuller, editor of the Democratic *Newark Journal,* who saw slavery as a matter of "states' rights," was astonished that anyone would wish to upset Newark's booming southern trade. In the November 1860 presidential election, Essex County slightly favored Abraham Lincoln, but he won only three of New Jersey's seven Electoral College votes.

When Confederate troops bombarded Fort Sumter, South Carolina, on April 12, 1861, volunteers for the Union army jammed the recruiting offices in Newark. Many impatient Essex men joined faster-moving units being formed in New York. Livingston, which was little more than an amalgamation of cross-

I shall be able to do no more than to bow to the people of New Ark from the train

A Lincoln

Astor House Feby. 19. 1861.

Despite opposition in Essex County and New Jersey in the 1860 election, President Lincoln agreed to "bow" as his train passed through Newark on his way to his inauguration. However, he had the train stopped and toured streets near the station, receiving cheering welcome. Courtesy the New Jersey Historical Society.

road hamlets, saw fifty-one of its young blades march off to war.

Newark City Counsel Theodore Runyon, thirty-eight-year-old newly commissioned brigadier general, led one thousand Essex men (mostly Newarkers) to Trenton on April 30. With an additional 2,123 men added in Trenton, Runyon marched down Pennsylvania Avenue in Washington on May 7 at the head of the first fully uniformed, fully equipped regiment to reach the nation's capital.

As the war intensified, the exodus of soldiers continued. Essex men were prepared briefly at hastily erected Camp Frelinghuysen in Newark before streaming off to southern battlefields. Enthusiasm for war ebbed as the casualties mounted, and, on July 13, 1863, when Lincoln announced a draft of able-bodied men, angry mobs rioted in Newark and Orange and pelted pro-Union newspaper offices with stones.

Thousands of Essex County people jammed the Orange railroad station on June 27, 1863, to greet General George B. McClellan, soon after Lincoln had removed him as Union commander. "Little Mac" bought a home on "The Ridge" in West Orange; from there he waged his unsuccessful fight against Lincoln for the Presidency in 1864—although McClellan did secure all seven New Jersey electoral votes.

While most of the business community of Newark and Essex County opposed the war, Marcus L. Ward stood firmly for the Union. His family, painted during the war by noted portraitist Lily Martin Spencer, took second place as Ward worked to establish hospitals for wounded soldiers during the war as depicted (facing page, top) in the New York Illustrated News. *At war's end, he was a leading force in establishing in Newark a home for disabled soldiers.* Frank Leslie's Illustrated Weekly's *artist was present on September 6, 1866, for dedication ceremonies (facing page, bottom). Ward was widely hailed throughout New Jersey as "The Soldier's Friend," a title that helped him win election in 1866 as governor of New Jersey.*

Orders for war material poured into Essex County factories: uniforms from Oakes woolen mills in Bloomfield, copper from Belleville, shoes and hats from Orange, and an array of manufactured goods from Newark's widely diversified plants. The one-time reliance on the South eased and had disappeared by war's end.

The two hundredth anniversary of Newark (and all the area that become Essex County) was celebrated in May 1866 by another of Newark's frequent parades. It was a time for boasting: only New York and Boston among major American cities were older. Forty of the original sixty-four founding families had descendants living in Newark or the adjacent Essex County suburbs.

Old Newark Township, which originally included the entire county area, had split into thirteen municipalities by 1870. Orange Township had been severely segmented during the war: South Orange (including Maplewood) had declared its independence in 1861; East and West Orange both seceded in 1863. Bloomfield, which had lost Belleville in 1839, saw West Bloomfield break away in 1868, declaring it now would be called Montclair.

Railroads made it easy to reach Newark jobs. Suburban wives rode the cars into the city for up-to-date fashion, for pleasant lunches in an increasing number of restaurants, and for matinee performances of popular plays. The completion of a street railway system in the 1860s—using genuine horsepower—became the

major factor in creating the famed Essex County suburbs, all dependent on Newark.

Horse-drawn streetcars had begun appearing on Newark streets on March 15, 1859, when the Orange and Newark Horsecar Railroad Company sent its first car into the city. By 1875, the little one-horse (sometimes two-horse) cars went nearly everywhere, clattering noisily over cobbled streets at a pace just faster than a man could walk. At four miles an hour, a ride from Newark to Tory's Corner in West Orange was not something to be taken lightly—even if it beat walking.

The horse railways used a riot of colors to identify routes. Multi-hued cars flashed by on Newark's streets—white to Newark's "Ironbound" section, dark orange to Irvington, blue to South Orange, red to Woodside, green to Roseville, and other colors to most of the county.

Newark was no longer off the beaten track. The city was alive, alert, and prosperous. In 1870, nearly seventy-five percent of

all county residents lived in the city. Each day thousands of suburbanites poured into Newark to work, to shop, to attend to financial matters, or to enjoy the city's many recreational opportunities.

Irked at being constantly cast in the shadow of New York, the city staged a major industrial exhibition in 1872. General

General George B. McClellan, relieved of command by Lincoln in 1863, built a home on "The Ridge" in West Orange and there ran an unsuccessful campaign against President Lincoln in 1864. Courtesy the Newark Public Library.

Theodore Runyon, former mayor of Newark and Essex County's Civil War leader, spoke warmly at the exposition of Newark's continued dominance in "old" manufactures (leather, carriages, beer, hats, clothing, varnish, and scores of other products), but stressed that much of the industrial growth also stemmed from new items—chemicals, hardware, thread, enameled goods and other products not known fifty years earlier.

Most of Newark's powerful industrial heads lived in the city, close to Military Park, partly because their factories were within walking distance, partly because of lingering traditions. A *Northern Monthly* magazine highlighted two of those traditions in the fall of 1867: Newark's still-evident Puritan mores and its remarkable shade trees. The writer noted the city had "a sacred stillness" on Sundays, nurtured in neighborhoods "almost embowered with green."

Banking and insurance stepped up to provide capital as the city's industrial base broadened. Newark became one of the nation's leading "insurance" cities when John F. Dryden founded the Prudential Insurance Company in 1875. It soon ranked with Mutual Benefit Life Insurance Company, founded in 1845.

Several outlying Essex County towns provided vacation retreats or "health resorts," featuring such benefits as the supposedly magical mineral spring in West Orange and much-touted healthful air in Montclair and Belleville. Inevitably, some of those who could afford to vacation in such areas decided they must live there year-around.

Served by the nearby Morris & Essex Railroad, luxurious country homes first appeared in Llewellyn Park, founded near Eagle Rock in 1853 by Llewellyn Haskell, a New York wholesale drug tycoon. Later, in 1877, Stewart Hartshorne, the wealthy inventor of the roller window shade, designed the winding, shaded streets of Short Hills, meant to be an "ideal community" and destined to become an exclusive enclave in Millburn Township.

Essex also became noted as a place where famed artists and writers found inspiration. Washington Irving frequented Newark as early as 1807. Frank Forester, a celebrated nineteenth century writer on outdoor life, spent his most productive years on the outskirts of the city. Mary Mapes Dodge, author of *Hans Brinker*,

Dr. William O'Gorman of Newark served during the Civil War as chief physician at Fort Monroe on the James River in Virginia. He became president of the New Jersey Medical Society in 1876. Courtesy the Newark Public Library.

or the Silver Skates, lived in the southwestern part of Newark. Asher B. Durand of Jefferson Village (now Maplewood) and George P. Inness (Montclair) were celebrated American painters. Many writers and artists lived in The Enclosure in Nutley.

The concentration of handsome estates in the Essex suburbs attracted well-educated women, most of them married to wealthy entrepreneurs. They put idle time to work for the benefit of their communities, and in 1872 the Woman's Club of Orange became the first woman's club in New Jersey and the fourth in the United States.

Also in Orange, rebellious Lucy Stone became an outstanding leader in the emerging fight for women's rights. She married Henry B. Blackwell but kept her maiden name. She refused to pay local taxes because women were not represented in fashioning the levy.

Two more Essex municipalities were formed in 1874. The people of old Camptown renamed their village Irvington, and Franklin Village withdrew from Belleville. Later, in 1902, Franklin became Nutley.

Busy, thriving, progressive: Essex leaders constantly used such adjectives to describe their county in 1880. Factories beside the railroads grew larger and more substantial; the many new red brick manufacturing plants, mostly steam powered, gave Newark a "red tinge." Exclusive homes in the suburbs became *de rigueur* for the wealthy.

It was a time of smugness, of a belief that there was little that could be added to better reflect the seeming prosperity. But just on the horizon were changes of such extent that anyone mentioning them would have been considered slightly daft.

A black-edged broadside advised New Jersey mourners when to expect the Lincoln funeral train on April 24, 1865, as it bore his body home to burial in Illinois. Thousands of weeping people crowded along the tracks as the train passed through the eastern edge of Essex County. Courtesy the Newark Public Library.

NEW JERSEY RAILROAD & TRANSPORTATION CO.

SPECIAL ARRANGEMENT

FOR THE TRANSPORTATION OF THE REMAINS OF THE LATE

PRESIDENT ABRAHAM LINCOLN,

OVER THE NEW JERSEY RAILROAD,

On Monday, April 24, 1865,

UNDER INSTRUCTIONS FROM THE WAR DEPARTMENT.

A Pilot Engine will precede the Special Train, leaving each Station 10 minutes in advance of that train.

THE SPECIAL TRAIN WILL BE RUN AS FOLLOWS:

STATIONS	TIME	SPECIAL INSTRUCTIONS
Leave New Brunswick at	7.55 A. M.	No Train or Engine (except the Pilot Engine) must enter on the main Track for New York, or leave any Station within 20 minutes in advance of the Special Train.
Leave Metuchen at	8.07 A. M.	
Leave Rahway at	8.35 A. M.	No Train or Engine must enter on the main track, or leave any station until 20 minutes after the Special Train has passed.
Leave Elizabeth at	8.55 A. M.	
Leave Newark at	9.20 A. M.	No Train or Engine must pass over Passaic Bridge, either way, between 9.05 A. M. and 10.00 A. M., unless both the Pilot Engine and Special Train have passed.
Arrive at Jersey City at	9.50 A. M.	Telegraph Operators must be at their stations and report the arrival and departure of the Special train to all stations.
Due at New York (by Ferry Boat) at	10.00 A. M.	

A Pilot Engine will precede the Special Train, leaving each Station 10 minutes in advance of that train.

F. WOLCOTT JACKSON, Gen'l Sup't.

J. W. WOODRUFF, Ass't Sup't.

When Civil War veterans gathered in Chicago in June 1868, these four Essex County men were there. Standing were Major William W. Morris and Major David Ryerson; seated were Colonel Tay and Colonel William Ward. Courtesy the Newark Public Library.

Like Livingston, the Caldwells, and other parts of Western Essex, Roseland was little more than a dot on a map in the 1860s, but after the Civil War it raised this substantial monument to those who had left their plows to join the Union forces. Courtesy the Newark Public Library.

A crude wooden porch fended off rain and snow at the Morris & Essex Railroad's Orange station at South Day Street in about 1860, when a heavily male crowd awaited an incoming train. Courtesy Orange Public Library.

Outward from Newark, or close to railroad tracks in the suburbs, there were many open areas, such as the sparsely settled Doddtown section of East Orange, surrounding Springdale Lake, when this photo was taken in 1872. Courtesy Richard E. Condit, East Orange photographer.

The passage of two decades after the war did not erase the natural beauty in suburban areas. Charles Warren Eaton, a noted Montclair artist, painted this scene in 1887, close to the center of Bloomfield. It later became Watsessing Park. Courtesy the New Jersey Historical Society.

Bloomfield's secluded town green, circa 1865, did not foretell the large town about to burst along Broad Street, Bloomfield Avenue, and nearly every other side street. In the distance is the Presbyterian Church. Broad Street is to the left, Liberty Street to the right. Courtesy the Newark Public Library.

"The Quarry" in Llewellyn Park, West Orange, circa 1870, showing sandstone ledge on Glen Avenue as it descends into the glen. Courtesy the Newark Public Library.

Waterwheels continued to turn nearly all local gristmills and sawmills until well after the Civil War. By the 1890s such millwheels as this at Smith's Mill in Millburn, once the power that made some of Millburn's noted paper, was lapsing into a romantic reminder of days long past—a victim of cheaper, more reliable steam engines. Courtesy the Newark Public Library.

The colorful, historically accurate mural in the Maplewood Municipal Building includes Pierson's Mill as it looked in 1875, when a small farm surrounded the mill. Courtesy the Township of Maplewood.

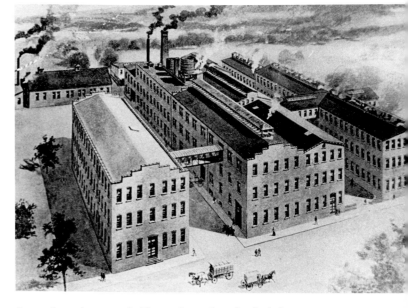

Responding to slurs, real or imagined, that Newark was "only a workshop," the Board of Trade opened its stunning Industrial Exhibition in August 1872, in the town Skating Rink, and for two months showed off work of the city's artisans and craftsmen. Courtesy the Newark Public Library.

A Northern Monthly *writer in 1867 called Fagin & Company's flour mill on the Passaic River in Newark "the largest of its kind in the world." It was ten stories high, produced 2,400 barrels of flour daily, and commanded a splendid view. Here, two party boats are tied up at Fagin's dock.* Northern Monthly Magazine, 1867.

Orange hatmakers earned widespread attention after the industry began in the Orange Valley as early as 1790. The foremost name, Stetson, began in the 1820s and by 1875 had built this substantial factory incorporated as No Name Hat Manufacturing Company. The Stetson hat of Western fame might have been more difficult to sell as "The No Name Hat." Courtesy the Orange Public Library.

The age of electricity was only dawning and even the use of steam was not usual as the 1880s and 1890s moved along. Strong backs and eagerness to work made the difference. On the previous spread, Ballantine's Brewery workers toasted their product, their important industry, and themselves. A gang laid paving stones (below) in Orange and men unloaded building materials (right) on the Passaic River docks in Newark. Paving scene, courtesy Orange Public Library; Ballantine's and dock, courtesy the Newark Public Library.

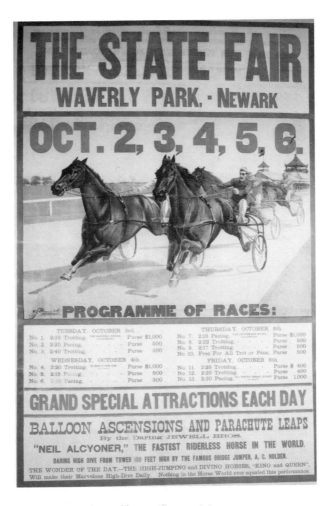

THE STATE FAIR
WAVERLY PARK · NEWARK
OCT. 2, 3, 4, 5, 6.

PROGRAMME OF RACES:

TUESDAY, OCTOBER 3rd.
No. 1. 2:35 Trotting. THE WAVERLY STAKE Purse $1,000.
No. 2. 2:25 Pacing. - - - - Purse 500
No. 3. 2:40 Trotting. - - - Purse 300

WEDNESDAY, OCTOBER 4th.
No. 4. 2:20 Trotting. IN AID OF THE FAIR Purse $1,000.
No. 5. 2:15 Pacing. - - - - Purse 500
No. 6. 2:35 Pacing. - - - Purse 300

THURSDAY, OCTOBER 5th.
No. 7. 2:19 Pacing. THE OVERBROOK STAKE Purse $1,000.
No. 8. 2:22 Trotting. - - - Purse 500
No. 9. 2:17 Trotting. - - - Purse 500
No. 10. Free For All Trot or Pace. Purse 500

FRIDAY, OCTOBER 6th.
No. 11. 2:29 Trotting. - - - Purse $ 400
No. 12. 2:25 Trotting. - - - Purse 400
No. 13. 2:30 Pacing. THE NORTH JERSEY STAKE Purse 1,000

GRAND SPECIAL ATTRACTIONS EACH DAY

BALLOON ASCENSIONS AND PARACHUTE LEAPS
By the Daring JEWELL BROS.
"NEIL ALCYONER," THE FASTEST RIDERLESS HORSE IN THE WORLD.
DARING HIGH DIVE FROM TOWER 100 FEET HIGH BY THE FAMOUS BRIDGE JUMPER, A. C. HOLDEN.
THE WONDER OF THE DAY.—THE HIGH-JUMPING and DIVING HORSES, "KING and QUEEN",
Will make their Marvelous High-Dive Daily. Nothing in the Horse World ever equaled this performance.

No event topped the annual State Fair at Waverly in Newark. Families saved pennies the year around to experience the thrills of what they considered to be the best in entertainment as well as a chance to see the finest in farm produce and livestock. As this 1885 broadside indicated, the fair management made a special appeal to adults (mainly males) who wanted to see trotting races. There was no sanctioned betting, but unofficial bookies catered to those with change to wager. Courtesy the Newark Public Library.

It wasn't all work and no play. Harper's Weekly caught both the obvious court action and the intended social significance of the crowd at Orange Lawn Tennis Club in July 1886, when the New Jersey State Lawn Tennis Association held its first tournament. The Orange club was one of the first to accommodate both men and women. Harper's Weekly, 1886.

In the 1880s a transplanted Canadian, Dr. Francis J. E. Tetrault, introduced the sport of tobogganing to New Jersey by building a third-of-a-mile-long slide on the slope of First Mountain in West Orange. Harper's Weekly, 1891.

Education in private academies had been commonplace in most of Essex County since colonial times. Benjamin Franklin School, the first public school in East Orange, was built on Dodd Street in 1823, when the town was still part of Orange Township. The school cost taxpayers $233.33. Courtesy the Newark Public Library.

(Above) Hats were the rage when Millburn scholars posed, presumably during a baseball game (the boy in left foreground has a bat). The school stood in the 1880s at the corner of Old Short Hills and Parsonage Hill Roads. Courtesy the Newark Public Library.

(Left) James Baxter, one of the foremost African-American educators in the nation, came to Newark from Philadelphia in 1864 to run the city's Negro School. The first black girl was admitted to Newark High School in the 1870s, but when Baxter died in 1909, all Newark schools were open to all children. Courtesy the Newark Public Library.

Many eighteenth century people educated themselves in libraries. South Orange Library patrons of the 1890s had to climb stairs that took them above Beck's Paint and Hardware Store on South Orange Avenue. The age of libraries as community centers had not yet emerged—nor had Andrew Carnegie unleashed part of his fortune to build solid monuments in several parts of the county. Courtesy the Newark Public Library.

Seton Hall College, a struggling little Catholic college, moved from Madison to this campus in South Orange in 1860. Ninety-five years later, it became Seton Hall University, a major New Jersey and national institution. Courtesy the Newark Public Library.

The first home of today's prestigious New Jersey Institute of Technology was at 21 West Park Street, Newark. Started in 1883 as Newark Technical School, the building was too narrow for all students to stand in front. Courtesy the Newark Public Library.

This etching of Orange in the 1800s focused on a wide (if unspecified) street, the large neat houses, picket fences, sidewalks, towering trees, and a lady strolling with a parasol—and called it suburbia. And so it was, with residents fully aware that they enjoyed a natural link to urban Newark. Courtesy the Newark Public Library.

Although middle class Newarkers proclaimed they moved westward to seek more room in the last decades of the nineteenth century, they tended to build their substantial houses close together, as in the fashionable area of Glenwood and Park Avenues, East Orange. Contrastingly, when the picture was taken of wide open spaces close to Williamson and Belleville Avenues, Bloomfield, the area had just begun to be filled in with more and more homes. Courtesy East Orange Public Library.

Suburbia needed such amenities as fire protection. The first firehouse of the Montclair Hook & Ladder Company No. 1 in 1884 included a watchtower that afforded a 360-degree view of the entire town. Courtesy the Newark Public Library.

Orange Memorial Hospital started in this three-story, Queen Anne style building, not a converted home but rather a structure planned and built in 1882 as a hospital. The adjoining structure, opened soon after, housed the first nurses' training school in New Jersey. Courtesy Orange Public Library.

Armed only with fierce looks and billy clubs, this Irvington Police force kept the peace in the 1880s (facing page). A major job was making sure that doors and windows were locked on such businesses as John N. Crawford's grocery and dry goods store attached to the Crawford home. Courtesy Irvington Public Library.

An awareness of antiquity had begun by 1895, when the venerable Johnson Homestead was in its 125th year. When built in 1770, the address was 72 Broad Street, Newark. After the Civil War, that was changed to 199 Clinton Avenue. Courtesy the Newark Public Library.

Local fruits and vegetables, all harvested on nearby farms (including some within city limits), graced the produce store on the corner of Newark's Springfield Avenue and Rankin Street in 1885. In an age of advancing specialization and a quest for leisure time, increasing numbers of people did not bother to plant even a backyard garden. Courtesy the Newark Public Library.

This print of Livingston's center in about 1885, made from an obviously faded glass plate, is more historically vital than photographically excellent. Sam's Tavern, on the right, hosted Livingston's first town meeting in 1813. A. W. Harrison's store, looking here like something in an early western mining town, served much of western Essex County throughout the nineteenth century. Courtesy the Newark Public Library.

The Orange Crosstown and Bloomfield Railway Company featured on its letterhead its business hallmark: a horsedrawn streetcar that ran north and south to connect suburban towns rather than heading into Newark in the manner of most streetcar lines. Courtesy Orange Public Library.

During the 1870s and 1880s, horsedrawn streetcars such as this pioneering model on the Belleville-Newark run provided relatively fast, safe movement through suburban Essex County and along the increasingly busy streets of Newark. Courtesy the Newark Public Library.

A horsedrawn streetcar plodding south on Broad Street in about 1890, perhaps on a Sunday morning considering the lack of traffic. The new Prudential building is in the center background, and Old First Presbyterian Church towers above the trees on the right. Courtesy the Newark Public Library.

Thomas Alva Edison, likely the most prolific inventor in history, came to Newark in 1871 at age twenty-four and lived in Essex County for all but six years until he died in 1931. Usually shown as a very old man, he posed here in 1878 with the phonograph he invented at Menlo Park in nearby Middlesex County, where he remained until he moved his operations to West Orange in 1883. Courtesy of Wide World Photo.

CHAPTER 4

IDEAS, MUSCLES, AND MONEY

Thomas Edison, a twenty-four-year-old telegrapher and fledgling inventor, arrived in Newark in the winter of 1871, seeking skilled hands and space to manufacture his newly patented, improved stock ticker. Western Union had bought the ticker for $40,000, enough to rent the top floor in a four-story building at 4–6 Ward Street. Within a month Edison had spent most of his capital on machinery.

Edison was scarcely noticed in 1871. By then, Essex County had gained national attention for its industrial prominence, particularly Newark, where a community of fine minds and daring spirits pioneered new ideas, built huge new factories, and improved products that had been traditions almost as old as the city itself.

Edward Weston, brilliant Newark inventor of many electrical devices, "lit up" part of Essex County with his generating plant, (right), won national fame for his voltmeter patented in 1899, and was world-acclaimed in 1931 for his "electric eye," widely used in photography. Courtesy the Newark Public Library.

Manufacturing soared, particularly in Newark, where such traditional industries as leather, jewelry, paint and varnish, clothing, and machinery grew stronger and increased in size. One of the major changes came in the city's powerful beer industry.

German brewers with such surnames as Krueger, Feigenspan, and Wiedenmayer came to the area to supply lager beer to growing German populations in Newark and Irvington. Not to be outdone, Peter Ballantine, the Scot who started a Newark brewery in 1840 to make ale, acquired a rival brewery in 1873 and added lager beer to his output.

Bigness was the rage. George A. Clark, a Scot who arrived in Newark in 1864 began the trend, erecting a huge factory in northern Newark in 1866. Four years later, one thousand men and women spun Clark Thread, trademarked O.N.T. ("Our New Thread").

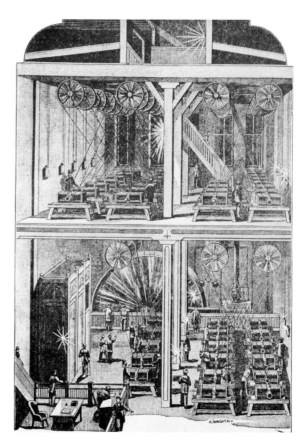

John Wesley Hyatt followed, building a five-story factory in 1873 to make celluloid, a plastic he had developed in Albany, New York. He perfected an injection molding machine to make huge quantities of such wares as combs, knife handles, piano keys, and a wide variety of specialized items useful to the area's industries.

Jewelry makers, who had flourished in the city since before the Revolution, shunned the trend toward bigness. Scores of small firms continued to fashion delicate rings, necklaces, and brooches in small lofts. However, the cumulative sweepings from their floors sent enterprising Edward Balbach on his way to riches in a big business in refining precious metals.

Balbach arrived from Germany in 1850 and built a refinery to extract gold and silver from the floor sweepings. By 1875, he was refining $5 million worth of precious metals annually—as much as the United States Mint.

The refinery benefited Newark doubly. As an offshoot to the

gold and silver, it produced pure lead, vital to the city's vigorous paint industry. Success with the previous metals also induced two platinum makers—Daniel W. Baker and Charles Engelhard—to open refineries in the city in 1875. As a result, Newark became the heart of America's platinum industry.

In 1876, Edison took his carefully assembled crew off to start an "invention factory" at Menlo Park in Middlesex County, vowing to achieve "a minor invention every ten days and a major one every six months." In Menlo Park, he invented the phonograph, an instrument for recording and playing back sound; perfected the incandescent lamp; and instituted a system of distributing electricity that made him world famous.

Edison's departure from Newark had given Edward Weston, an English-born inventor, the opportunity to flourish after he settled permanently in Newark in 1875. In 1877, he established the world's first electrical machinery plant in a former synagogue on Washington Street.

Weston lit up the Newark scene after the city hired him in 1877 to install five brilliant arc lamps in Military Park, the nation's first municipal-financed street lighting. By 1884, his patents covered the entire electrical field from motors and generators to underground cables, batteries, and fuses. Arc lamps were

Madness at Broad and Market Streets in Newark in 1885, when horse-drawn streetcars, buggies, freight wagons, and mobs of people vied for space on the streets. The organization of Public Service Corporation in 1903 was intended to end the chaos, but by 1910, an amazing total of 552 electrically driven trolleys (nearly ten a minute) were scheduled to pass Essex County's key intersection every hour. Courtesy the Newark Public Library.

85

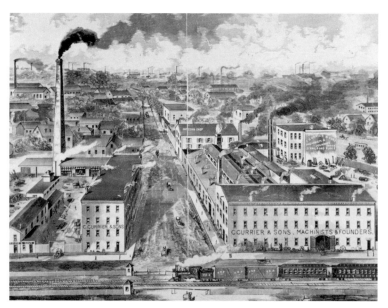

By 1890, when an artist featured the huge machine shops and foundry of C. Currier & Sons, smokestacks dominated the skyline in the "Down Neck" area of Newark. Later, elevation of the Pennsylvania Railroad tracks created an embankment that gave the area a lasting name: The Ironbound. Courtesy the Newark Public Library.

While Newark wrestled with the problems of frenzied traffic and limited space, rural life remained strong in Essex County in the 1890s, as evidenced by the barns, milk wagons, horses, and hay fields of Dorer's dairy farm near Stuyvesant and Lyons Avenues in Irvington. Courtesy the Newark Public Library.

far too costly (and perhaps deemed too dangerous) for the rest of the county; only a few Essex towns had even installed gas street lights before 1880.

Beyond Newark, most villagers lived much as they and their ancestors had for 150 years. The 1880 Census showed that 136,508 of the county's 189,959 residents (seventy-two percent) were Newarkers; only Orange (13,207) topped 8,500 in the other twelve municipalities. Livingston, Franklin (Nutley), Millburn, and Irvington all had fewer than two thousand residents.

The bucolic nature of the backlands can be seen through a description of Montclair in 1876, which was remembered by Dr. S. C. G. Watkins as "composed of farms" about to be cut up for building lots. He recalled Montclair had "great fields and large old orchards around every place, as this had been a great apple country, where each fall great quantities of cider were made" for shipment throughout the nation.

Orange had prospering hat and leather industries; by 1890 the small city's hatters averaged more than five million head coverings annually. Millburn's papermills continued to make quality paper and the Oakes Wool Mill in Bloomfield had become one of the nation's foremost makers of woollen cloth for uniforms. Belleville solidified its reputation as a fabricator of fine copper and brass products, and its quarries still supplied sandstone blocks for New York City's acclaimed "brownstone" mansions.

West Orange took pride in its

fashionable summer clientele. The visitors rode into town in "handsome equipages drawn by stylish looking horses." The town reportedly had "a lively appearance at certain hours of the day." Visitors soon demanded better roads; in the summer of 1868, blasting began in nearby Second Mountain to supply trap rock for the roads. It was a major, if short-lived, industry.

West Orange, and all of the industrial scene in western Essex, was about to explode. Thomas Edison returned to the county in 1887, choosing West Orange for his huge new laboratory and manufacturing complex. The choice was dictated in some measure by Edison's decision to install his second wife in the posh surroundings of Llewellyn Park. His laboratory would be within walking distance of the Edison home; the inventor would continue his research there until his death in 1931.

Edison soon erected a multi-storied factory adjacent to the laboratory to manufacture storage batteries, phonographs, records, and other products. By 1908, the West Orange company had made and sold 1.5 million phonographs and 100 million cylinder records.

While this scene in Millburn is less than a century old, the intersection at Main Street and Millburn Avenue in 1905 could have been pre-Civil War. A horse-drawn vehicle passes another in the foreground. In the background a haywagon awaits the horsepower trotting its way. Courtesy the Newark Evening News.

The quest for good health led young Llewellyn Haskell, New York wholesale drug tycoon, to build a rustic home, "The Eyrie" (or Eagle's Nest) on the precipitous slopes leading downward from Eagle Rock, a noted landmark in Pre-Civil War days. Haskell broke ground in 1852 and gradually expanded his health-restoring retreat into a section for very wealthy people.

Edison initially concentrated on motion picture development in West Orange, both in the "Black Maria" (the world's first recording studio he built to make indoor movies) and in the varied terrain surrounding the laboratory. The first moving picture with a plot, *The Great Train Robbery*, was made in 1903 on or near area railroads. As a result of this film, however primitive, Edison-made nickelodeons materialized everywhere. One film historian wrote, "Overnight the movies became the poor man's theater."

Frank Sprague, one of Edison's associates at Menlo Park, built a major factory at Bloomfield in 1892 to make electric hoists, fans, and motors. The Edison laboratory was only two miles away. Soon a large triangle of land—extending from the Edison works to Sprague's factory to a flag stop called Crescent (later Ampere) on the Montclair Branch of the Delaware, Lackawanna & Western Railroad and back to Edison's plant—became the focus of the nation's prime regions for makers of electrical products.

The crucial need for industrial expansion in 1890 was capital, not genius. Most towns had small banks, usually formed to underwrite the businesses of their directors. They could not, or would not, finance large projects. Newark's insurance companies stepped into the void; by 1895, the city ranked fourth nationally in insurance assets, topped only by Hartford, Philadelphia, and New York.

Mutual Benefit Life Insurance Company, founded in 1845, and the Prudential Insurance Company, started in 1875, led the way. John F. Dryden founded the Prudential on a new philosophy: give working men life insurance at an

Haskell's development, Llewellyn Park, featured isolation and security from its founding in 1853. The gatehouse shown here was a spire, an architectural detail in Haskell's home. Rough roads were built through the park to preserve as much pristine atmosphere as possible. The development attracted many well-known, wealthy people, including Thomas A. Edison.

Stewart Hartshorne, who invented the device that made window roller shades practical, used some of his fortune to purchase land in Millburn Township, well off the beaten track. There, in 1877, he established Short Hills, meant to be an "ideal community." These early Short Hills homes were quickly enhanced with lush shrubbery and shade trees. The area today is one of New Jersey's most exclusive addresses.

affordable price. The "Pru" (as it was familiarly known) had sold more than one million policies by 1890 and more than eleven million by 1912. Hundreds, then thousands of young men and women flocked into Newark to work in the impressive new buildings that Prudential completed in 1892.

Electric streetcars bound the county together. However, the first experiments with an electrified street railway were made in Orange, not Newark, as might have been expected. The Orange Crosstown Railway tried electric power in the spring of 1889, but strong local opposition forced cancellation of the experiment within two months. Horses returned to pulling the cars. Orange also had the county's first cable cars, designed to haul cars to a mountaintop hotel. The railway worked but the hotel failed.

Newark capitalists invested in cable power on the Newark & Irvington Street Railway in 1888, without success. However, on October 4, 1890, electrified Car No. 1 rode up Court House hill in Newark using full electrical power. Trolleys became the rage. They sped people to new home developments outside of Newark, suburban workers to their city

In the beginning, Short Hills was a long carriage drive from the Millburn railroad station, a deterrent in attracting the upscale New York and Newark businessmen that Hartshorne believed would enjoy the carefully-planned development. Hartshorne built a depot close to his property, induced the Delaware, Lackawanna & Western Railroad to stop in Short Hills, and his community thrived.

jobs, Sunday excursionists to amusement parks in Belleville and Irvington, baseball fans to games in Weidemeyer Park, and musical enthusiasts to concerts in Schuetzen Park.

Trolleys pulled Essex County together, but two other factors helped. For one thing, three Newark department stores reached out for wealthy suburban matrons, even as they catered to city shoppers. The three, Hahne's (dating back to 1858), L. S. Plaut

(founded 1870), and L. Bamberger & Company (started in 1892), were easily the finest department stores in all of New Jersey.

A second factor was the founding of the *Newark Evening News* in 1883. The *News* deliberately reached beyond city limits from the start, reporting suburban news heavily and turning a nice profit from suburban interest in

One house, wide open fields, and hundreds of parasols to ward off the midsummer sun formed the rural setting for a spectacular 1893 hot air balloon ascension in Irvington. A few spectators lounged on the green pastureland, but most stood for the hour of preparation before the launch. Courtesy the Irvington Public Library.

In this photograph, undoubtedly posed for publicity purposes, Thomas Edison uncharacteristically paused for relaxed reading on the lawn of Glenmont, his home in Llewellyn Park. His office and research laboratory were about a mile away in Orange Valley. Courtesy the Newark Public Library.

the advertising by Newark stores, theaters and restaurants. The *News* acquired a national reputation for its thorough coverage, good (if somber) writing, and its constant vigilance on city and county affairs.

Newspapers reflected the rise of leisure time. The western hills became in wintertime a place for winter sports. In summer, tennis courts in Orange and Montclair reflected the popularity of a relatively new American sport. The Passaic River became a major boating mecca on both banks of the waterway.

No endeavor surpassed baseball, the nation's first genuinely democratic sport—easy to learn and easy and inexpensive to play. Every vacant lot by 1880 became a potential grounds for "the American pastime." One of the earliest fully documented games involved an Orange nine and the powerful Nassaus from Princeton College in 1863. They played to a 43-43 tie. Irvington's professional team won a reputa-tion for skilled, aggressive play in the 1880s and the predeces-sors of the Newark Bears began playing in 1883.

Recreation needed open lands. The most farsighted ven-ture of the period was establish-ment of the Essex County Park System in 1895—the nation's

Edison's major achievement in West Orange was perfection of motion pictures, particularly the development of cameras and projectors. Many of his films were shot indoors in the "Black Maria," built in 1893 and set on a track to permit rotating to get full sunshine. The "Maria" shown here is a reproduction built in 1954 by the National Park Service, current custodians of the historic site. Courtesy the Newark Public Library.

No place in small towns was more vital than the general store located somewhere near the town center, such as the Philip Doremus store on Bloomfield Avenue, Montclair. A professional camera-man included everything in his "portrait" of the family hold-ings—the store, the Doremus home on the right, and the one-horse delivery wagon. Storekeepers usually lived behind or over the store or right next door. Courtesy the Newark Public Library.

first. Opponents claimed that buying land when there was plenty of open space everywhere wasted taxpayer money. The park commissioners explained that they sought to save some of that space

for future generations. The commission established parks in several parts of the county and bought two huge "reservations" atop Second Mountain, then virtually a wilderness.

The county park commissioners were part of a new breed emerging as the nineteenth century blended into the twentieth: enthusiastic supporters of education, hospitals, libraries, museums, and aiders of people without money, friends, or hope. Volunteers became the unsung heroes and heroines of the day.

They included such people as William N. Barringer, Newark's forceful educator in the 1880s and 1890s; Randall Spaulding, superintendent of Montclair schools as that town expanded and modernized its educational system between 1874 and 1912; and James M. Baxter, a patient, magnetic teacher, who came to Newark from Philadelphia in 1864 to take charge of the city's "colored" school. When he retired in 1909, all Newark schools were integrated.

There was more enthusiasm for education in the large suburban towns than in Newark, despite the fact that the first high school in New Jersey, and third in the United States, was Newark High School (later Barringer). In 1900, that one high school was deemed sufficient for a city with a population of 246,000— at least twenty percent (about 50,000) of whom were of high school age.

Newark's public library, founded in 1888, became the shining jewel in the city's cultural crown when John Cotton Dana, arguably

Stores such as S. Moore's Fish & Oyster Market in Bloomfield's well-shaded center would today serve as the family's market. Such "fresh" items usually were not sold in general stores, and "Butter, Cheese & Eggs, Etc." could also be had here. Proprietors and workers alike posed in front of the shop and in the window above in 1893. Courtesy the Newark Public Library.

The workforce of Gentzel's Grocery Store in Millburn could offer almost anything in 1897, from the steam radiators in the front to Pioneer Mills "coffees & spices" that are advertised on the sign beside the clock. Most workers in such stores had lifetime jobs. Courtesy the Newark Public Library.

the nation's all-time finest public librarian, became its director in 1901. Until his death in 1929, Dana steered the library to greatness, and also found the time and energy to open the Newark Museum in 1909. Far smaller Montclair, growing rapidly as a commuter town, opened its new public library in 1904, and in 1909 began what was to become the Montclair Art Museum.

Higher education was in place. In South Orange, Seton Hall College celebrated its fiftieth anniversary in 1906. Newark Technical School, founded in 1881, grew toward college status (and attained it in 1918 as Newark College of Engineering). Newark Normal School, started in 1855, moved into a handsome new building on Broadway in 1913. Bloomfield College dated to 1869 (founded as Bloomfield Seminary). The need for high school teachers led to the opening of Montclair Normal in 1908, the same year that New Jersey's first law school was founded in Newark. Upsala College moved from Kenilworth to East Orange in 1924.

By 1910, Essex County's population had soared past the half million mark to 512,886. Newark led, of course, with 347,469 residents, but several major suburban towns had emerged: East Orange, benefiting from trolleys extending the reach of workers, had 34,171 residents, followed by Orange, 29,630; Montclair,

The Morris Building, an 1885 "mini mall," where nearly everything from groceries to hardware could be acquired— including newspapers sold at Hoe's Newsstand on the corner. The three stores were razed soon after to make room for Orange Savings Bank. Courtesy the Newark Public Library.

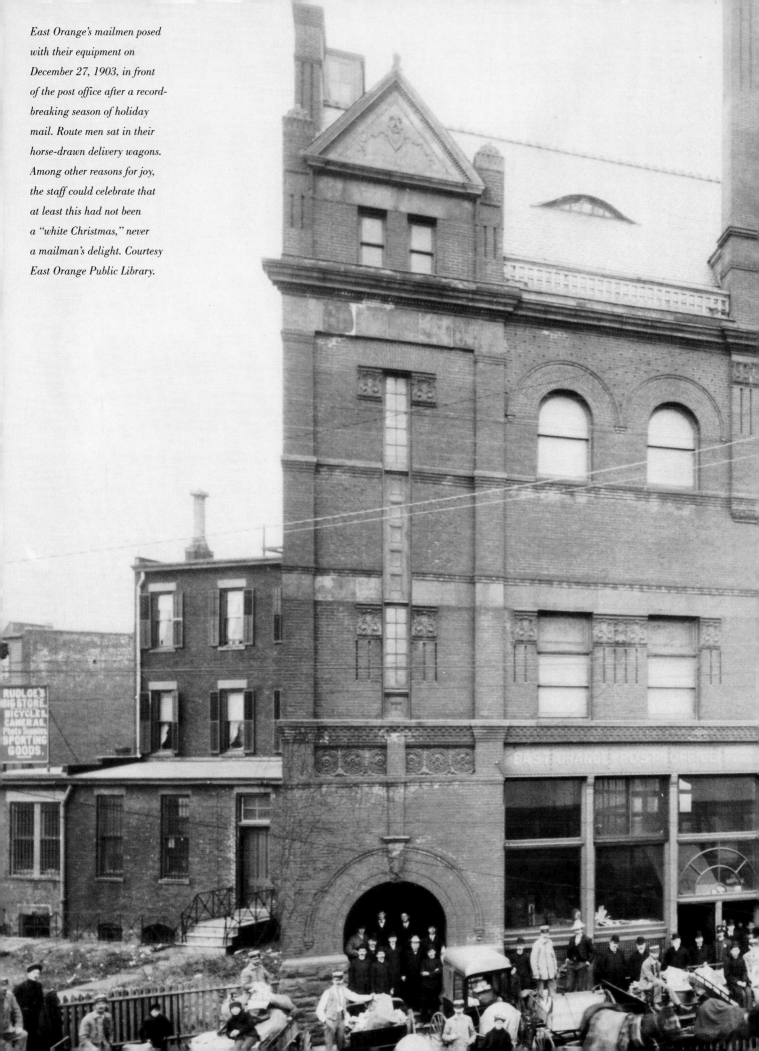

East Orange's mailmen posed with their equipment on December 27, 1903, in front of the post office after a record-breaking season of holiday mail. Route men sat in their horse-drawn delivery wagons. Among other reasons for joy, the staff could celebrate that at least this had not been a "white Christmas," never a mailman's delight. Courtesy East Orange Public Library.

21,550; Bloomfield, 15,070; Irvington, 11,877; and West Orange, 10,980.

Numbers told only a bit of the story. The strong Puritan influence lingered throughout the county until the 1890s. Newark had welcomed large numbers of German and Irish immigrants in the 1840s and 1850s, and Irvington had assimilated many Germans. Orange had many Irish settlers. By 1900, these early immigrants and their sons and daughters had become part of community power.

By 1900, too, the great influx of immigrants that brought "new people" (from southern and eastern Europe) was well underway at Ellis Island. Those newcomers settled in clearly defined and severely limited areas, as demonstrated in a 1911 map of Newark that featured "areas where different nationalities predominate." Italians, Jews (mostly Russian), and Germans comprised about sixty percent of the city's estimated 235,000 immigrants.

Black residents ("Negroes" on the map), lived close to Broad Street. Large colonies of Jews, Irish, and Italians shared the hillside west of the city center. The Ironbound, cut off from the rest

One of the defining maps of Newark, drawn in 1911, clearly delineated the city's ethnic divisions. National and social groups were not totally together; there were, for example, four enclaves of Germans, four of Italians, and three of blacks ("Negroes" on the map), all with similar religious, ethnic, or work interests. The German area in the southwestern part of the city was by far the largest. Courtesy the Newark Public Library.

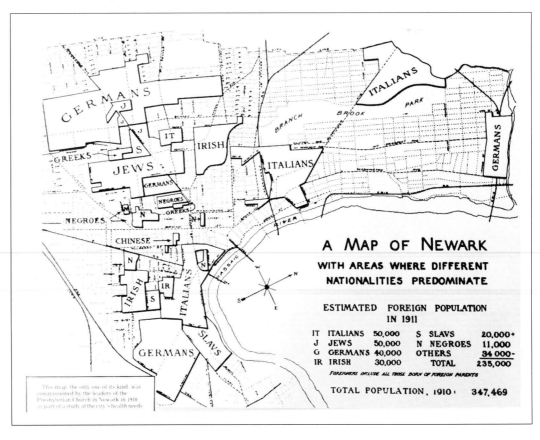

Scotland Road and South Orange Avenue, the center of South Orange Village in 1900, was the right location for Hose Company No. 1 and No. 2 and Hook and Ladder Company No. 1, all reliant on horse-drawn equipment. The pseudo-Tudor building with a Swiss-like fire watchtower is now the Village Hall. Courtesy the Newark Public Library.

Courtesy the Newark Public Library.

Increasing numbers of Americans sought outdoor recreation in the 1890s. Thus, one of Essex County's most notable achievements was the formation of the nation's first county park system in 1895. The thickly settled area near the old city reservoir in northern Newark, shown as it was in 1896, became Branch Brook Park. Today the entire area is either woodland or lawns. Conversely, South Mountain Reservation, set aside in 1895 for future use, is if anything, wilder than when photographed in 1895.

of Newark by the high embankment raised for the Pennsylvania Railroad, was inhabited mainly by Irish, Italians, Germans, and Slavs.

A colony of Chinese lived in an area ("Chinatown") about three blocks southeast of Broad and Market streets and facing on Mulberry Street. They reminded some of a contingent of thirty Chinese men imported in 1870 to labor at the huge Passaic Steam Laundry in Belleville.

The years between 1880 and 1910 were the "twilight time" for the hectic and rewarding years that saw the changing of the nature and spirit of America. Across the Atlantic, Europe prepared for a war that would test the mettle of the western world. Choices would have to be made, particularly in the immigrant communities. Essex County—and all of America—would never be the same.

Courtesy the Newark Evening News

Recreation could be almost anything. A favorite was taking photos with better cameras and flexible film. The Orange Camera Club's outing on the Morris Canal in 1894 naturally motivated members to pose themselves. One club member sat on a mule, the mule driver sat on the other—a place he would never assume if on a job. Courtesy the Newark Public Library.

(Below) The corner pub was a major form of recreation, particularly in German and Irish neighborhoods. Seated perilously close to the swinging doors of Irvington's Stuyvesant House, two patrons are shown here offering a toast with Kastner's Lager Beer in about 1900. Wives and daughters looked on from upstairs windows. Courtesy the Newark Public Library.

Annie Oakley, "Miss Sure Shot," undoubtedly the most accomplished female star ever to appear in nineteenth century "Wild West" shows, lived most of her adult life in Nutley. She found living close to New York City was imperative for even those who portrayed the supposed lonely life under Western skies. Courtesy the Newark Public Library.

Montclair High School's 1893 football team, with just enough players to form a starting lineup, posed on the school steps with mustached Dr. John S. Gibson, faculty adviser. This was one of New Jersey's first high school football teams, in a time when players had no helmets or shoulder-guards and the ball was almost round. Courtesy Montclair Public Library.

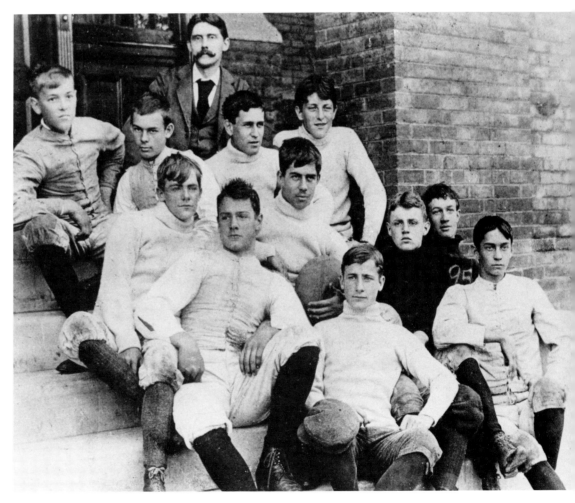

Recreation for little boys could be an adult's disaster, as when this 1903 flood on the normally placid Passaic River poured huge volumes of water into the streets near Belleville's Reformed Church. Courtesy the Newark Public Library.

It's easy to spot the loser in the match between these two would-be Orange tennis stars of 1905. Black stockings, knee-length pants, black sneakers, and bright neckerchiefs were in vogue on the courts. Courtesy Orange Public Library.

An unidentified couple posed in about 1900, he with derby hat, cigar, and camera, she in white with an elaborate black hat. The tree, seemingly held up only by its bark, and the little pond to their right, were well-known in Halcyon Park, a Bloomfield real estate development that promised buyers "the life of a millionaire" at a low price. Courtesy Bloomfield Public Library.

When Ira Kip built this stone mansion in 1903, it was totally in Montclair. Four years later, on establishment of Verona Borough, a realignment of municipal boundaries placed the front part of the structure in Verona, the rear in Montclair. That added to the aura of an unusual building long known as "Kip's Castle." Courtesy the Newark Public Library.

(Above) Boys meeting girls is never a mystery, but where was the fourth bicycle when this well-dressed foursome, supposedly on a cycle tour of Essex County, met in a shaded Montclair glade in the late 1890s? A rage for cycling struck the county and the nation during these years as the century ended. Courtesy the Montclair Public Library.

Irvington and Maplewood's Olympic Park, an outgrowth of an earlier German gathering place for singing and picnics, became a magnet for young people throughout most of the nineteenth century. The grove-like appearance in the early 1900s gradually was replaced by thrill rides, a swimming pool, and other amusements. Courtesy the Newark Public Library.

The Glorieux family lived the good Victorian life in their three-story Irvington home in the early twentieth century. The house and family provided background for the family's carriage and splendid team of horses. Courtesy the Irvington Public Library.

William Cone, dean of Essex County photographers, posed the Daniel Colton family at the turn of the century in a socially correct afternoon tea. Surprisingly, to a modern viewer, the garden scene was in the very center of Newark, on Park Place across from Military Park. Reaction of the young man to the daily ritual can only be imagined. Courtesy the Newark Public Library.

Veterans of the Spanish-American War marched north on Broad Street in 1900, shortly after their return from Cuba and Florida, but the major Essex person in the Caribbean adventure was Clara Louise Maass, born in East Orange, educated in her early years in Livingston, and prepared for nursing at Newark German Hospital. She became one of America's great heroines in 1900 when she became the first American—and the only woman—to die in experiments in Cuba that proved Yellow Fever was transmitted by mosquitoes. Courtesy the Newark Public Library.

Enthusiasm for the deeds of distant ancestors accelerated early in the twentieth century. Showers did not dampen spirits on June 14, 1907, when the Dispatch Rider monument was dedicated in the churchyard of Old First Presbyterian Church in Orange. Courtesy the Newark Public Library.

Coal was the fuel of choice to provide the steam for factory engines and to heat residences in 1911 when John Blondel & Son of Montclair promised "discrimination to the family." Blondel's sixteen horses delivered the coal, and wagon drivers sought to honor the company's promise to deliver the black diamonds "with no damage to lawns or flower beds." Courtesy the Newark Public Library.

A classic immigrant portrayal was this scene along Newark's Jewish Prince Street at the turn of the century. Crowds from nearby tenements mingled with bargain hunters from outside the district. Courtesy the Newark Public Library.

John Cotton Dana, one of America's greatest librarians, became director of Newark Public Library in 1902, just as swarms of immigrants were flooding into the city. Dana encouraged them to read, advertising the library in seven languages. In his twenty-seven years at the helm, the library became the intellectual and cultural center of Essex County. Courtesy the Newark Public Library.

Dana's closest friends included Louis Bamberger, founder of the notable Bamberger's Department Store, called "one of America's great stores." Here Bamberger (in light suit and cane) is shown on a California vacation in the 1920s with his brother-in-law and sister, Felix and Carrie Fuld. Bamberger and Fuld became New Jersey's most powerful merchant princes and, as their fortunes mounted, the most generous philanthropists. Bamberger donated funds to build Newark Museum and endowed the internationally known Institution for Advanced Study in Princeton, whose residents have included Albert Einstein and T. S. Eliot. The Fulds donated the nucleus of the spectacular blossoming cherry trees in Branch Brook Park in Newark and Belleville. Courtesy Ellen B. Defranco, Los Angeles, California.

Proof that historians are correct if they talk or write about "a small army of men" working in the early twentieth century is this photo of such an "army" preparing a trolley right of way by removing old pavement on Springfield Avenue in Irvington. They were newly arrived immigrants, agreeable to taking any job that offered a foothold in this country. Courtesy the Newark Public Library.

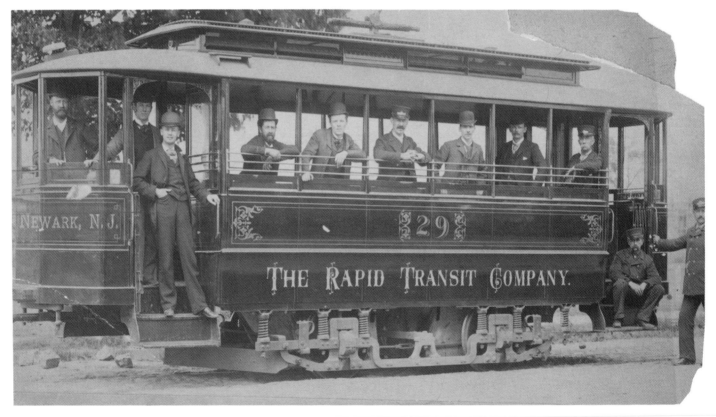

One of the earliest Essex County electric trolleys was Number 29 of the Newark Rapid Transit Company. This might have been the first ceremonial run, since only motormen and derby-hatted company officials were aboard. Electric street cars such as this were followed by even larger cars. It was the trolleys that bound the county together. Courtesy the Newark Public Library.

Trolley lines feared Second Mountain until the Eagle Rock Line conquered it. This car ran for more than three decades before being retired in 1924. Courtesy the Newark Public Library.

One of the tiniest trolley terminals was in South Orange, dignified by a red tile roof. Trolleys stopped, seats were turned around, and the car headed out on the way back to the wonders of Newark. Courtesy the Newark Public Library.

*Magnets for shoppers through-
out Essex County were Newark's
"big three" department stores—
Hahne's, pictured at holiday
time just before World War II;
Bamberger's, shown in the 1920s,
and Plaut's, whose window
in this case showed samples of
"25,000 corset covers, gowns,
skirts, drawers, and corsets," all
on sale in about 1910. Courtesy
the Newark Public Library.*

One of the places that appealed to suburban visitors to Newark was James De Jianne's North End Restaurant at 447 Broad Street, "an oyster and chop house" of about 1895 that catered to "Ladies & Gents." Upstairs, a dentist waited for customers. Next door, an ice cream soda cost five cents. Courtesy the Newark Public Library.

The streetcars also helped move the work force to their jobs, particularly women who for the first time began to find jobs other than in textile mills or housecleaning. Lined up as if for inspection, white-garbed cooks and servers proudly showed off the stoves and kitchen equipment used to prepare meals for Orange school pupils in the early twentieth century. Courtesy the Newark Public Library.

No Essex County employer had a greater female working force than The Prudential Insurance Company. It depended on female clerks (and male supervisors) in the 1890s and far beyond. The "Pru" was considered an ideal place to work, although females were required to resign if they married. Courtesy the Newark Public Library.

The most critical point in trolley history came at this grade level crossing of train and trolley tracks on Clifton Avenue, Newark. Here, nine high school students were killed and thirty injured on February 19, 1903, when a trolley car's brakes failed to hold. The car crashed through the crossing gates into the path of a speeding train. A week later, a train still sped through the intersection, but public outrage soon caused the elevation of railroad tracks throughout the county. Courtesy the Newark Public Library.

(Facing page) Laborers clung to the sides of old wooden passenger cars on the work train that in 1913 carried them outward in the meadowlands, where they dug drainage ditches for emerging Port Newark. Courtesy the Newark Evening News.

Many plans for improved docking facilities at Newark had come and gone, but early in the twentieth century ships still disgorged their cargoes (including the Rockefeller oysters being unloaded here) much as they had since the founding of the city. A red-letter day for Newark, Essex County, and the East Coast on October 20, 1915, brought a well-dressed crowd to the dedication of newly built Port Newark. A few days later, the four-masted schooner, A. J. West, moved out of Newark Bay and into the port to make it a working reality. Courtesy the Newark Public Library.

This new home of the Fireman's
Insurance Company in the heart
of Newark was finished in 1910
to replace the company's older
headquarters. The sixteen-story
structure launched Newark into
the "skyscraper age." Equally as
important in the minds of many
historians and architects, razing
the old building (shown below)
robbed Newark of one of the
nation's most handsome Victorian
business landmarks. By 1910,
most of the ugly overhead wires
had disappeared, and a few
automobiles were on the streets.
Still, trolleys predominated and
horses were still in the running.
Courtesy the Newark Public
Library.

Bus service came to the western part of the county before it became usual on the streets of Newark. William L. Kerris, who ran a horse-driven stage between Caldwell and Pine Brook, replaced that vehicle with this sturdy Mack sightseeing bus in 1909. This and its followers doomed trolley service everywhere. Courtesy the Newark Public Library.

Top-hatted and handsomely dressed VIPs, looking every inch the part of the dignitaries they were, rode in open phaetons to lead Newark's 250th anniversary parade down Newark's Broad Street in 1916.

High enthusiasm greeted the entry on April 6, 1917, of the United States into the war against Germany.
"Newark's Own," the 312th Infantry, started from Washington Street on May 14, 1918, and marched
down Broad Street to the train that took them to Hoboken and quick shipment to France. Of 3,000
Essex men in the regiment, 550 died and 1,800 were wounded. Courtesy the Newark Public Library.

THE YEARS
OF TESTING

Communities surrounding the mother city of Newark in 1910 had the slightly superior feeling that
they were "the suburbs," reliant upon the city but
comfortably removed from urban problems: streets overhung with
telegraph, telephone, and electric wires; traffic snarls; old neighborhoods succumbing to decay; and a severe testing of every
facility and every custom.

Yet, could suburbia be East Orange, with 34,371 residents
or Orange with 29,630; Montclair with 21,550 or Bloomfield,
with 15,070? Beyond those four towns, Essex County remained
rural, although sounds of the future could be heard: the automobile was bringing suburbia closer, but it was still on the horizon
for awhile.

CHAPTER 5

Another Essex County draft contingent is off to war, headed out of Newark on September 5, 1918, aboard a Central Railroad of New Jersey train. Their introduction to army life would be basic training at Camp Humphries in Virginia, but the war ended before they were ready for battle. Courtesy the Newark Public Library.

Newark itself was barely a city in 1910. The aging, seldom-used Morris Canal, a relic of the 1830s, flowed through the very heart of town. Eighty-five miles of Newark streets were unpaved. Railroads had just completed the elevation of their tracks through Newark and Essex County, prompted when a speeding train rammed a trolley at grade-level in February 1903, killing nine high school students.

Thomas N. McCarter Jr. organized the Public Service Corporation of New Jersey in 1903, vowing to bring order to both street traffic and the highly competitive gas and electric industry. By 1910, he admitted that the situation at the Four Corners (Broad and Market Streets) remained intolerable: 552 trolleys (about ten every minute) passed the intersection during a peak hour.

Downtown Newark was rising, literally. In 1910, the Fireman's Insurance Company demolished its old Victorian home office and replaced it with a sixteen-story, gleaming white "skyscraper." Across the street (where town founder Robert Treat had built his home), the twelve-story Kinney building rose in 1912. Nearby, Prudential finished its trio of sturdy Gothic

In a little-known facet of World War I, the United States used the Big Piece Meadows in western Essex (near Caldwell Township) for target practice in 1918. The area there was isolated and desolate. Courtesy the Newark Evening News.

buildings in 1909. Immediately north and south, like a pair of ecclesiastical bookends, Trinity Church and Old First Presbyterian Church served notice that antiquity was still honored.

Most city businesses and social leaders lived in town before World War I, clustered in spacious homes around Military or Washington parks or in fine mansions on High Street. A few wealthy businessmen had begun to move to fashionable enclaves out along the Lackawanna Railroad—to Llewellyn Park in West Orange, Short Hills in Millburn, or beyond to the millionaire regions of Morristown and Somerset Hills.

Essex County was in reality "larger Newark." Leading suburbanites made their money in the city. Well-to-do suburban women were driven to Hahne's department store in Newark, as carefully protected as if they were stage actresses. Young suburbanites frequented society affairs in the city. Working people enjoyed the city lights, and rode a trolley at least once a year out to Becker's Grove (later Olympic Park) in Irvington or Pleasure Park (later Riviera Park) in Belleville.

And then it was over, "Over There." Flags fluttered on high, crowds jammed the thoroughfares, and trollies and cars moved slowly on Broad and Market Streets on Armistice Day, November 11, 1918. Most Newarkers turned out to publicly welcome the return of peace. Signs like the one on the Kinney Building, "Give to the United War Work Drive," would soon fade into memories. Courtesy the Newark Evening News.

The entire county could join in celebrating three major happenings:

❑ Opening of rapid train service directly into New York City first via the Pennsylvania Railroad tunnel to Pennsylvania Station in 1910. A year later, the Hudson & Manhattan Railroad (known as "The Tubes"), began a twenty-minute service from downtown Newark to uptown Manhattan. That service was another reason to live in Essex County.

❑ Opening of Port Newark on October 20, 1915, after forty years of dreaming and about two years of digging. Newark, Essex County, and all of New Jersey now had an outlet to the Atlantic Ocean.

❑ Celebration of the 250th anniversary of the founding of

Newark, starting on May 1, 1916. It was a time for people in Bloomfield, Belleville, the Oranges, Montclair, Irvington, and elsewhere to remember from whence they came.

Gloom crept across the county in 1917, dampening all celebration. The European War grew worse; when Americans died on liners torpedoed by German submarines, tension neared the breaking point.

As a counterpoint, a war boom engulfed the county. By June 1916, nearly $20 million had been invested in Newark's Down Neck factories. Particularly impressive was the rise of the chemicals industry in the Meadows. Every other county factory of any size knew the pleasant jingle of dollars for the tools of the European War.

The declaration of war by the United States in April 1917, was not a surprise. Young men rushed into recruiting offices.

The cheering stopped. Towns held memorial services, paused for a minute at 11 A.M. every Armistice Day, and more lastingly, erected monuments, such as this doughboy statue in Verona. Courtesy the Newark Evening News.

The Essex County National Guard was federalized. Members of West Orange's proud Essex Troop rode their horses off to war. Those who stayed home worked in the booming factories and at the Submarine Boat Company at Port Newark, where as many as seventeen thousand employees produced 118 prefabricated freighters before the war ended.

Casualty lists saddened the county, but an even more devastating and immediate event struck in the autumn of 1918 when an awesome influenza epidemic broke out. Newark reported the first sixteen cases and one death on September 27. By October 10, more than 1,500 new cases were reported daily in Essex County. Four days later, Newark alone reported 1,626 new victims.

No part of the county was spared. The flu struck rich and poor, young and old, suburbanite and city dweller alike. Schools

The wounds healed quickly. Only a few years before this, Newarkers had marched up Broad Street in virulent anti-Kaiser protest. Now, around 1930, German Ambassador Baron V. Prittswitz shook hands with Newark Mayor Jerome T. Congleton. In the background, reception committees of the American Legion and area German-Americans formed an honor guard. Photograph by Drew B. Peters Studio, courtesy Donald M. Karp.

and theaters were closed. People in stores and public offices wore masks. When hospitals were full, YMCAs, clubs, public buildings, and vacant structures throughout the county became temporary hospitals before the epidemic was declared officially over on November 12. By then, nearly 35,000 county residents had been felled. About 1,500 of them died.

Bells tolled the end of World War I on November 11, 1918. Troops began arriving home the following May to welcoming parades, promises, and joy. Most Essex County communities approved plans for memorials, erected the statues, and moved on to enjoying the boom times that buoyed the nation.

The Twenties sped along euphorically. As the decade began, horses and carriages were almost as numerous as gas-driven buggies. A few curious residents enjoyed the radio broadcasts that began on June 1, 1921, from Station WJZ in a Newark studio. Motorists welcomed improvements on several highways that weaved through the county—such as Bloomfield Avenue, Mt. Pleasant Avenue, and Springfield Avenue—but the feeling of genuine road progress did not come until 1932, when the local portion of the notable New York-to-San Francisco road (Lincoln Highway) was finished through Newark.

The suburbs finally came of age in the 1920s. Rows of modern shops appeared in the main streets of Montclair, East Orange, and South Orange. Town pride, often fostered through successful athletic teams, grew intensely. Elementary schools were improved, a few high schools were built. Buses began to replace streetcars.

The age of boosterism swept across Essex in the 1920s. In 1929, the Newark Airport management proudly announced that four thousand passenger flights were booked for the year. Montclair's boosterism took a different track, following an article written in 1922 that extolled the town as "an artistic Parnassus on the mountainside" in trib-

As another gesture to a World War I participant, this time Russia, an ally, a freighter stood by at Port Newark in 1922, awaiting relief supplies for a nation torn by war and internal revolution. The port had grown mightily during World War I. Courtesy the Newark Evening News.

By 1922, when the distinguished choir of Bethany Baptist Church helped the church celebrate its fiftieth anniversary, thoughts of war had faded for most Essex County people. Faded Foliage, Amorel E. O'Kelly Cooke.

ute to the many artists and writers who called Montclair home.

Two of the county's newest and least populated towns, Glen Ridge and Essex Fells, eschewed self-promotion. Glen Ridge broke away from Bloomfield Township in 1895, the fifth municipality to be formed from old Bloomfield. Essex Fells quietly withdrew from Caldwell Township in 1902. Both towns became havens for well-to-do residents who generally shunned the spotlight.

Glen Ridge won wide attention for its nonpartisan "New England town meeting" type of local government and its careful regulation of buildings, from the stone railroad depot to a controlled shopping area. By 1925 it was a far cry from the 1870s when it was known as "Moffett's Mill" and little more than a stop on the railroad.

Optimism filled the area. Ignored was the crushing automobile traffic that choked business centers. Nearly everyone disregarded Prohibition, which was the law of the land. Illegal speakeasies were jammed to the doors and gangsters were idolized. Downtown Newark hailed the rise in the 1930s of huge new buildings—one as high as thirty-four stories. Electrification in 1929 of the Delaware, Lackawanna & Western Railroad through the Oranges, westward through Millburn and Short Hills, and to Bloomfield, Glen Ridge, and Montclair, tied the county more closely together.

Big industry eyed Essex County. The Hoffman-LaRoche Company of New York started the trend in a modest way in 1929. It bought a twenty-three-acre farm in Nutley that year and erected a single building. By 1941, Hoffman-LaRoche buildings spread over seventy-five acres on the Nutley-Clifton border, the growth spurred by the company's discovery and production of vitamins.

Suddenly, the Wall Street stock market collapsed in October 1929. Factories rapidly trimmed their employee rolls; many plants closed entirely. Banks failed. Stores reined in their inventories. The Depression brought misery and hardship, so deep that thousands of penniless people walked town and city streets in hopeless quests for

Traffic on Bloomfield Avenue (below) in Glen Ridge was relatively light, although a truck and trolley allowed little room for anything else on the Belgian block pavement. The gaslight beside the truck makes it easy to know this is Glen Ridge. In another Bloomfield Avenue scene in Glen Ridge (right), gasoline on this day in the 1920s was 10.9¢ a gallon. Courtesy Glen Ridge Public Library

Courtesy the Newark Public Library

work. By the middle of 1930, more than 37,500 persons in Newark alone were out of work.

Despite the severity of the Depression, movie houses prospered with double features and "gift nights." Restaurants survived with full-course dinners for fifty cents. With jobs scarce, high school enrollment picked up, and the one-time two-year "normal schools" became four-year teachers colleges. As a capstone, the 1937 Newark Bears of the International League were acclaimed by many sportswriters as the finest minor league team in baseball history. The Bears captured the 1937 International league pennant by a huge margin, winning 109 games and losing only 43.

As the 1930s wore down, the economic pace slowly accelerated, moved upward by war orders from England and France. It seemed like old times, like the years before World War I, complete to the feeling that the Atlantic Ocean insulated this nation from World War II. The dream evaporated on Sunday afternoon,

Repairmen for the Public Service Bus Company at work in 1924 at the company's Irvington repair shop. The buses of the 1920s were small and fragile in comparison with today's counterparts. The camera caused a work stoppage; every mechanic looked at the lens. Courtesy the Newark Evening News.

December 7, 1941, when radio announcers interrupted a professional football game to announce that Japanese planes had bombed Pearl Harbor in Hawaii.

Alarm and fear swept the nation, but amid those strong emotions, all traces of the Depression vanished. Factories displayed "help wanted" and "no experience necessary" signs. Nearly five thousand Essex County men and women volunteered to be air raid wardens. Thousands of others worked on draft boards, rationing boards, and other civilian by-products of war.

The famed Essex Troop had been in federal service for nearly eleven months by December 1941. The first of the nearly 140,000 Essex County men and women (80,000 from Newark) who would enter the armed services began swamping recruiting offices the day after Pearl Harbor. The nation was far more involved in a total war effort than at any time during World War I.

Women became a major force in the workplace for the first

time in history. They moved out of traditional clerking and bandage rolling to become riveters, welders, lathe operators, and to engage in many other kinds of physical labor that males had long felt were their province alone.

But the war casualty lists grew, week after week. Essex County men (and a few women) died in places that even few geographers could have identified before the war—Salerno, Bastogne, Anzio, Guadalcanal; Iwo Jima, Okinawa, and the Coral Sea. They were Christians and Jews, white and black, sons of the founders of Essex County and sons of first-generation Americans.

Enormous quantities of war material flowed from Essex County to the theaters of war—uniforms, shoes, food, instruments, airplane

Thomas A. Edison and unidentified friends arrived at the D.L. & W. Railroad station in Montclair in 1930 on the first electrified train on the line. The clean windows and dirt-free exterior of the cars would not happen again in the fifty-plus years these green cars ran on the railroad. Courtesy the Newark Public Library.

Even in 1922, when this picture was taken, the intersection of busy trolley tracks and the equally busy D.L. & W. Railroad was an anachronism at Main Street and Arlington Avenue, East Orange. In the center of the picture, two gate tenders stood by to crank the gates down by hand after the trolleys and other traffic had slipped past. Soon after, the railroad tracks were elevated. Courtesy the Newark Public Library.

parts, tents, telephone equipment, fuses, radios, surgical supplies, medicines, vitamins, and nearly everything needed to make the war machine operate. Two enterprises stood out: Federal Telephone and Radio Corporation and Federal Shipbuilding and Drydock Company (not interconnected despite the somewhat similar names).

Federal Telephone and Radio had come to Newark in 1931 as a tiny company, manufacturing parts for the International Telephone and Telegraph Corporation. Federal started expanding in 1941, taking over forty-four different locations in Newark and increasing its work force from a few hundred to 11,500 men and women. Federal was the nation's leading maker of field telephone equipment when it moved into its new plant in Nutley in 1943.

The federal government purchased the old and dilapidated Submarine Boat Company ways of World War I. Federal Shipbuilding and Drydock Company of Kearny ran the revitalized Newark operation. Peak employment of 19,053 men and women in October 1943, made good the company's boast that the yard "never sleeps." The Newark operation built seven destroyers, fifty-two destroyer escorts, and seventy-eight troop and tank landing ships.

Newarkers took on another big government war enterprise in 1942 when the Office of Dependency Benefits moved into a new Prudential building. ODB hired ten thousand persons in 1944, and mailed more than a half billion dollars in checks every month to military dependents throughout the nation. Twenty-six percent of ODB employees were black; for the first time, possibly anywhere, blacks were given the chance to fill varied and vital jobs.

Victory in Europe was wildly celebrated on May 5, 1945, in Essex County and everywhere else. Despite a steady rain, crowds jammed into every main street. But by noon most of the celebration had ebbed in an awareness that the struggle against Japan continued. Japan surrendered on August 15. This time fervor was unbridled—kissing, cheering, weeping, praying. The terrible years of war had ended.

Postwar readjustments came swiftly. The shipyard closed; more than fifteen thousand jobs vanished. The ODB pruned its payroll sharply, then dismissed the last of its ten thousand workers in 1945. Second and third shifts ended in nearly all factories. Impressive joint incomes earned in war by husbands and wives had to diminish. But on V-J Day, tomorrow could wait.

Opulence was in the air. In Short Hills, a caretaker showed off the rear of "Pleasant Days," the million-dollar estate of the late Joseph P. Day. The twenty-eight-room mansion cost more than a half-million dollars when it was built in 1914. It was elaborately landscaped with pools and lawns. Day was one of New York's leading real estate auctioneers. Courtesy the Newark Evening News.

Glen Ridge took proper pride in the 1920s in its ability to group all of the borough's stores in one location on Bloomfield Avenue near the municipal building. The Glen Ridge stores, erected in 1911, were a forerunner of early drive-in shopping centers. And, while the style of the patron's cars has changed, the store block remains attractive and valuable. Courtesy Glen Ridge Public Library.

The South Orange-Maplewood School District set out to build Columbia High School to be one of the best in New Jersey. It is shown under construction, shortly before it was completed in 1927. The school quickly became a state leader in academics, a winner in athletics, and a beacon of what a high school should be. Courtesy the Newark Evening News.

Newark Airport, rising out of the meadowlands mud in 1928, scarcely generated confidence and certainly held no hint that one of the world's major airports would eventually soar far above this meager beginning as one small hangar, dubious-looking runways, and a location on a soggy moor. Courtesy the Newark Public Library.

The state's largest and most important newspaper, the Newark Evening News, didn't wait for Newark Airport to be world-acclaimed. Typifying its slogan, "Always Reaches Home," the News loaded papers on an airplane for delivery to the Jersey Shore resorts on August 14, 1929. Let it be noted that the plane was a sister ship to Charles Lindbergh's "Spirit of St. Louis." Courtesy the Newark Evening News.

Newark Airport, possessor of the nation's first hard surface commercial landing strip, was by 1931 "the busiest airport in the world." In 1934, TWA's "City of Newark" began overnight service to Los Angeles. In recent decades, Newark International Airport has been rebuilt several times by the Port Authority of New York and New Jersey, which leases and operates the facility from the city of Newark. Courtesy the Newark Public Library.

Employees of the first Airport Restaurant posed outside for the grand opening in 1931. Later, as Newark Airport expanded, the size and the fame of the restaurant grew. No longer just a "lunch and soda" shop, the old Newarker Restaurant in a later reincarnation became one of New Jersey's most fashionable places to dine—with or without an airplane ticket. Courtesy the Newark Evening News.

Courtesy the Newark Public Library.

Within a year after Newark Airport opened in eastern Essex County, Caldwell Airport began operations in the western end of the county. Local officials hailed the opening of the facility with the arrival of Texaco's No. 13 (left). The airport has grown to respectable size but never came close to being a major facility. The airport played host to many famous names in aviation, including Charles A. Lindbergh (above), who visited in the early 1930s. Courtesy the Newark Public Library.

Essex Mountain Sanatorium, (right) set on one of Essex County's highest elevations, provided the clean air and country rest that were major factors in treating tuberculosis in the early years of the twentieth century. It became a haven for World War I veterans who had suffered lung injuries. In this photo, taken in 1934, the Sanatorium had become a very large institution. Courtesy the Newark Public Library: The Moore Studio.

Any kind of work brought joy, including such long-time jobs as building the Pulaski Skyway, connecting Newark with Jersey City. The opening on November 24, 1932, shown here, connected the state's two largest cities on a bridge that rose high over the meadows and the Hackensack and Passaic Rivers. Courtesy the Newark Public Library.

This hole in the ground in about 1930 would dramatically improve Newark. The area had been the bed of the unsightly, abandoned Morris Canal. The trolley system known as Newark City Subway was constructed in the hole, which was then paved over to create Raymond Boulevard, named for the late Mayor Thomas Lynch Raymond, Newark's most progressive mayor. Courtesy the Newark Public Library.

Long-awaited Pennsylvania Station was opened in 1935 as a massive facility for linking trolleys, buses, and the Newark City Subway. Penn Station now stands in the middle of Newark's impressive Gateway Center, and serves as a focal point for public transportation. Courtesy the Newark Public Library.

Irvington's fire tower and police pistol range were dedicated on chilly November 12, 1937. The tower has always been a landmark and since 1954 has been visible from the Garden State Parkway. Large portions of eastern Essex County had become heavily developed by 1937; increased fire and police protection were an important aspect of daily life. Courtesy the Newark Public Library.

By 1935, when these job seekers lined up outside the Newark Armory, the Great Depression had forced hundreds of factories to close. Many thousands of workers were unemployed. No section of the county escaped the crippling economic times. Courtesy the Newark Public Library.

Workers spent many months improving South Mountain Reservation and other parts of the Essex County Park system during the Great Depression. They felled trees, built roads and walks, cut underbrush, erected bridges, and built retaining walls. Elsewhere, WPA workers built post offices and schools and aided the county tremendously. Courtesy the Newark Evening News.

Not everyone was wretchedly poor. The Orange Lawn Tennis Club opened its outdoor swimming pool in 1933. Newspapers described the club as "the playground for society." Courtesy the Newark Evening News.

The 1920s and 1930s were a time to seek pleasure. Some found it outdoors, by hiking to the outlook at Eagle Rock in West Orange. There, protected only by a flimsy fence, they could enjoy a view that has captivated many people for at least two centuries. Courtesy the Newark Public Library.

No Lincoln's Birthday was real without the annual photo of Newark schoolboys "spontaneously" posing with the famous seated statue of Abraham Lincoln in front of the Essex County Court House. It was sculpted by Gutzan Borglum, also known for his four faces of the presidents in South Dakota as well as other Newark sculpture, including Military Park's Wars of America memorial. Courtesy the Newark Public Library.

The Verona Canoe Club team of Verona Park, winners of the second annual triangular regatta staged by the Essex County Park Commission at Branch Brook Park. Their opponents were teams from Weequahic and Branch Brook Parks. Courtesy of Charles DeMarco: Drew B. Peters Studio.

Baseball historians generally regard this 1937 Newark Bears team as the finest minor league team of all times. Described in spring training as "young, eager, and inexperienced," the team sped through the 1937 schedule with 109 wins and only 43 losses in winning the International League pennant. The Bears then whipped Columbus, Ohio, champions of the American Association, to win the "Little World Series." Sixteen of the seventeen regulars on the '37 Bears went on to play for major league teams. Courtesy the Newark Public Library.

Also significant in Newark baseball history were the Newark Eagles, champions of the Negro Baseball League in 1946. Their leader was third baseman Ray Dandridge. Courtesy the Newark Public Library.

Velodromes in Newark and Nutley brought the world's greatest cyclists to Essex County in the 1920s and 1930s. Here, famed rider Frank Kramer of Newark is shown as he prepared for his last ride in 1922. The races were especially popular among German-Americans and Italian-Americans. Courtesy the Newark Public Library.

Bands, flags, pretty girls, and handsome
men: parades are welcome in good times
and bad. World War I veterans led the
march that dedicated the new municipal
building in East Orange in 1929.
Belleville's popular Political and Social
Club's Fife and Drum Corps featured
the town's centennial celebration in 1939.
Belleville's municipal building was heavy
with flags for the occasion. Courtesy
the Newark Public Library.

German-Americans suffered from anti-German bias during World War II. At Irvington, as the war approached, a store owner offered $500 to anyone who proved that he and his family were not loyal Americans or were Nazi sympathizers. Courtesy the Newark Evening News.

The valorous Essex Troop rode off to war in 1941 on horses and trained at Fort Jackson, South Carolina. It was the first American cavalry unit to reach England when it arrived in October 1942. Using tanks rather than horses, the Essex Troop was in the invasion force on June 6, 1944, and fought their way across Europe until V-E Day. Courtesy the Newark Evening News.

In 1942 this building served as state headquarters for the state's OPA fuel rationing operations. Today the same building, located on the edge of Washington Park, Newark, is the state headquarters for the Veterans Administration. Courtesy the Newark Evening News.

The Sonny Dunham Orchestra enlivened a USO fund-raising effort on Newark's Broad Street in July 1941. Such events were common on city streets during World War II. Courtesy Handy and Boesser.

The message was big and clear on this billboard in Newark's Military Park, supporting the war efforts of the local Community Chest. Such billboards also promoted the sale of War Bonds. On the home front, civilians saved paper, cooking oils, tin cans, and scrap metal of all kinds that might be useful in the war effort. San Giacomo Paper manufacturers of Orange picked up "Scrap Going to War" in Livingston (below) and many other places.

Courtesy the Newark Evening News

Courtesy the Newark Public Library

There were thousands of Essex County factories, large and small, but lasting impressions came from big ticket items such as this bomber propeller being inspected in the Caldwell plant of the Curtiss-Wright Corporation. Courtesy the Newark Evening News.

Around the clock, seven days a week: workers at Federal Shipping and Drydock revered the facility's nickname, "The Yard That Never Sleeps." Before World War II ended, Federal's Newark Yard built seven destroyers, fifty-two destroyer escorts, and seventy-eight troop or tank landing ships. Employment peaked at 19,503 in October 1943. Courtesy Federal Shipbuilding and Dry Dock Company.

The Newark YWCA sponsored "Sunrise Dances" to afford soldiers and war workers the opportunity to meet. Thousands of people were thrown together for the first time in the war effort. From this picture, it appears "war workers" meant women and from the eight stags in front, it would seem there weren't enough war workers to go around. Courtesy the Newark Public Library.

They aren't "Rosie the Riveter," but these were among the thousands of female shipyard workers who could make anything or do anything. At Port Newark on May 30, 1943, these women were the first to fasten life nets on a newly launched destroyer escort at the Federal Shipyard. Courtesy Federal Shipbuilding and Dry Dock Company.

CHAPTER 6

AMERICA'S URBAN LABORATORY

On the Fourth of July in 1948, two little boys hang on the iron fence surrounding abandoned Christ Episcopal Church in Belleville. Built in 1836, when the nation was only sixty years old, the church was a sturdy symbol of the past. Courtesy the Newark Sunday News.

In 1946, a rooster crowing to usher in the dawn or cattle lowing at twilight would not have been unusual in Essex County, except in Newark or the larger suburban towns. Even on the outskirts of those populous areas, traces of rural life persisted. Belleville and Fairfield had extensive vegetable farms, Roseland was called "the Essex dairy country," and growers of horseradish lingered in the northern area of Bloomfield.

Massive changes were about to overtake, in some places even overwhelm, Essex County. The war had made people restless and the GI Bill of Rights gave veterans an unprecedented opportunity to own homes and to further their education. Thousands of veterans with long heritages of city life used government-backed mortgages to move into development homes in the western and northern sections of the county.

A major blow to Essex County agriculture came in the early 1950s when the Plenge family sold its Belleville vegetable farm to real estate developers. Several generations of Plenges had worked the farm, but the then-stupendous offer of $1 million for the twenty-five-acre farm was too much to resist. It was only a matter of time before the cows of Roseland, the horseradish of north Bloomfield, and the vegetables of Fairfield also gave way.

Newark remained the grand old dame of Essex County, however shabby and rundown in places (which many attributed to the war), but still lively and attractive. Downtown Newark glowed with the vigor of its department stores, its many movie houses, scores of first-class restaurants and theaters where big-name bands and famous entertainers performed. The city was considered safe and exciting, day or night.

Outward from the city center, industry managed to prosper in Newark and elsewhere—on one shift a day rather than the hectic around-the-clock feats of World War II. Few heads of Newark industry then envisioned moving to the suburbs. Unemployment could be felt, particularly among those people who had migrated to the city to find war work—a warning signal for all American cities.

The 1950 census confirmed that Newark's population was on the rise, up to 438,776, a jump of about 9,000 since 1940. More tellingly, it also showed that for the first time more people lived outside Newark than in it—the 467,173 suburban residents outnumbered Newarkers by 28,383.

Orange celebrated its 150th anniversary on November 25, 1956, with a parade down Main Street. The bands, floats, and marchers were observing the fact that Orange Township declared its independence from Newark Township in 1806. Courtesy the Newark Public Library.

East Orange had earned an unofficial nickname by the middle 1950s: "Apartment house center of the East." They came in all sizes and many heights. Dryden Gardens on Park Avenue, (above) with the "Williamsburg-like" center, was one of the then-increasingly popular "garden apartment" complexes. Ten-story "Fulton Towers" on Harrison Street (below, right) tried the high-rise look. The four-story apartment building (facing page) featured a "Middle East" decor. Courtesy the Newark Public Library.

As the GI-dominated move westward gathered impetus in Essex, newcomers to suburbia expected all of the amenities of a city—sewers, sidewalks, transportation facilities, downtown shopping areas, good schools, and professional police and fire departments. As hard-pressed communities raised taxes to meet such demands, most new residents sadly realized that many of the burdens and the taxes of urban living had followed them.

Livingston typified the new reality. The large township at the start of World War II could best be described as slow-paced farm country, closer to nineteenth century ways than to twentieth—the kind of place to pass through on the way to somewhere else.

Route 10, the old Mount Pleasant Avenue (and the one-time turnpike), carried most east and west traffic through Livingston in 1946. Huge chunks of open land lay along all of the township's other major roads. Four small, aging elementary schools were widely scattered through Livingston's fourteen square miles. High school students were bused to Caldwell and West Orange.

Livingston was home to about 6,000 in 1940. Ten years later, there were 10,000. Then the postwar boom struck: an additional 14,000 people moved in between 1950 and 1960. By 1960, in the midst of the "baby boom," Livingston's population stood at 23,124. All of the old elementary schools had been enlarged and six new elementary schools, two junior high schools, and a new high school had been built.

Within the next decade, Livingston became the essence of suburbia. St. Barnabas Hospital left Newark and built a new hospital in the township. One of New Jersey's largest malls rose at the junction of Eisenhower Parkway and South Orange Avenue. (Another major mall rose in Short Hills, just over Livingston's southern border.)

Essex County's colleges were overwhelmed by students seeking admission, thanks to the GI Bill. All colleges and universities had very large GI populations. Seton Hall led: ninety-four percent of its students were returned veterans. Seton Hall grew on those veterans; it attained university accreditation in 1956.

Enrollments swelled at Bloomfield, Upsala, and Caldwell Colleges. The most startling transformation came to four institutions: the two small teachers colleges in Montclair and Newark; respected (and small) Newark College of Engineering; and the difficult-to-know Newark University, a loose federation of little-known colleges in the city.

Montclair State Teachers College had seventy-five acres on which to grow, but Newark State Teachers College was crowded

Those aren't Barbie dolls seated in the center of the "dish," no matter how tiny they look seated on the "dish antenna" that the International Telephone & Telegraph Company of Nutley pioneered and erected at its Nutley plant in 1960, nine years before the United States landed on the moon. The antenna was intended to hear sounds bounced off the moon or from artificial satellites in space. Courtesy the Newark Public Library.

in its "school in the garden," built in 1912 on less than two acres. Montclair began its meteoric growth after receiving a 1951 state allocation of $4.7 million for buildings. (It became Montclair State University in 1994, with an enrollment of more than fifteen thousand students, about eighty percent of them commuters.)

Newark Teachers College opted to spend its $3.7 million state grant to build an entirely new campus in Union on the former Kean family estate. The college was renamed Kean College of New Jersey in 1972. (Not incidentally, that mere $3.7 million to build a college from scratch shows the value of a dollar in 1957.)

Highly respected Newark College of Engineering, hoping for long-delayed city and state aid, crowded the veterans and other students into outmoded buildings. Generous funding began in the late 1970s and 1980s. The college, renamed New Jersey Institute of Technology, was transformed into a modern institution.

Metamorphosis was the word for struggling Newark University after it was blended into Rutgers, the State University, in 1946. Buildings on Newark University's widely scattered "campus" included a former brewery, an ex-stable, a one-time razor blade factory, a former insurance company office building, and the one-time Newark YWCA.

Those scattered, disparate buildings, plus the relatively few students and the small faculty of Newark University, became the nucleus of Rutgers-Newark (as it was originally known). By 1960, a consolidated Rutgers campus had begun to rise on the hill west of downtown Newark. It would become the nation's largest college on urban renewal land. Students and faculty members were mostly commuters from surrounding towns. Adjacent to the Rutgers campus, Essex County College became another educational force in the county.

Workers at all levels, from chief executive officers to clerks, poured into Newark each day as the 1950s wore into the 1960s, doubling the city's population during daylight hours. Before World War II, most commuters had ridden trains or railroads into the city. Increasingly, postwar workers drove their automobiles to work, exacerbating already severe traffic and parking problems.

New Jersey's first genuinely "super" toll highways—the New Jersey Turnpike and the Garden State Parkway—both went through Essex County. The Turnpike, finished in 1953, and the Parkway, completed in 1954, would prove to be both a boon and a burden.

The boon was easy access to the outside world, particularly to the Jersey Shore. Negatively, all Essex communities suffered when residents followed the toll roads south to settle in Middlesex and Monmouth Counties; that exodus south and west was in full swing by 1960. That year, for the first time in the twentieth century, the county population declined—by only six thousand people, but nevertheless an augury of things to come.

Business and industry also edged away from Newark in the 1950s, often skipping entirely out of New Jersey to the warmer southern states, but often just heading to Morris County or beyond. Fortunately for Newark, the major headquarters companies stayed in place—the Prudential Insurance Company, Mutual Benefit Life Insurance Company, Public Service, New Jersey Bell Telephone Company, and several of the state's largest banks.

The value of open land in the Essex County Park system became more apparent as time sped by. The Eagle Rock and South Mountain reservations were augmented by an accumulation in the 1950's of 1,205 acres of mostly wetlands along the Passaic River in Livingston, Roseland, West Caldwell, and Fairfield.

Two county park structures built on a small portion of land in West Orange broadened the system's functions. The first, in 1958, was South Mountain Arena, a fully enclosed skating rink; followed in 1963 by Turtle Back Zoo, a lively, imaginative complex designed for children. The rink and zoo were overnight successes.

Bloomfield (1962) and Livingston (1963)

South Mountain Arena, opened in 1958 by the Essex County Park Commission, gets more publicity for its top-level high school and college hockey programs, but each year thousands of skaters—from beginners to national competitors—frequent the rink. The ice is often in use for eighteen or more hours daily at the height of its season. Courtesy New Jersey Newsphotos.

The Turtle Back Zoo, opened in 1963 by the Essex County Park Commission in the South Mountain Reservation in West Orange, has become a popular children's zoo for visitation as well as for education through area school use of the facility. Courtesy the Newark Public Library.

celebrated 150th anniversaries; both were preludes to Newark's year-long 300th birthday party in 1966. Amid the banquets, parades, athletic contests, and red-white-and-blue banners, there was the feeling that Newark was still a fine city, on the surface, at least.

Newark's population stood at 405,220 in 1960, down some from its all-time high of 438,776 in 1950, but that caused no alarm in City Hall or elsewhere. The insurance companies and banks still made the city the financial capital of New Jersey. New high-rise apartments in the northern part of the city were built to attract middle-class families. Newark remained the center of major department stores and first-run movie houses.

Suddenly, in July 1967, the facade crumbled. Long-ignored dissent of slum area residents boiled over into four days of rioting that rocked the hillside west of downtown. Twenty-six people were killed, hundreds more injured and millions of dollars of damage was inflicted on the neighborhood. The image of a peaceful, progressive urban center was torn away, revealing anger and discontent.

The flight from the city accelerated. The 1990 census revealed that more than 125,000 people had left town since the riots. Ironically, the exodus was facilitated by completion of two interstate highways through town in the early 1980s: Interstate 280 through the northern part of Newark's business section and Interstate 78 through the heart of the once-heralded Weequahic section (former home of noted author Philip Roth) in the southern part of the city.

The outward flow did little for the rest of Essex; the county population plummeted to 778,206 in 1990, the lowest since the mid-1920s. The interstates, intended to bring new residents and commerce to urban areas, proved to be yet another blessing and curse—and ultimately spread urban problems to rural counties, where ex-city residents continued to seek the elusive and likely

St. Barnabas Medical Center, opened in Livingston in 1964, was founded in Newark just after the Civil War. After nearly a century on Newark's High Street, St. Barnabas moved to Livingston when a survey in the early 1960s showed that about seventy percent of the hospital's patients came from west Essex suburbs. Courtesy the Newark Public Library.

nonexistent Utopia of high municipal services and low taxes.

The attractions of Essex County, a genuine laboratory for urban America, are still considerable. Count the blessings of a fine system of county parks, a network of good college campuses, a consistent dedication to cultural pursuits, widely varied municipalities, and more than three centuries of history and tradition.

Essex County architecture spans the centuries, from early colonial to federal, from neo-classical to Victorian, from late nineteenth century stick houses to the fine homes in Short Hills and Llewellyn Park, from the bungalows and "center hall colonials" of the 1920s to the split-level homes popular in the surge of GI mortgages.

There are, of course, two or three houses where Washington is said to have visited and the one house in Caldwell where Stephen Grover Cleveland, twenty-second and twenty-fourth President of the United States, was born in 1837.

This urban county has retained enough forestland and open water (thanks largely to the Essex County Park Commission) to be known for its natural beauty. There likely is no finer view in New Jersey than that from the lookout at Eagle Rock, in any season of the year.

Dedicated in October 1962, Temple Emanu-El left its Newark roots behind to build this startlingly beautiful and modern building in Livingston. On dedication day, folding chairs were used because permanent seating had not yet been installed. Courtesy the Newark Public Library.

The cultural tone of Essex may well center in The Papermill Playhouse in Millburn, opened more than a half century ago in the abandoned Diamond Paper Mill, a reminder of Millburn's beginnings. The Playhouse suffered a disastrous fire in 1980, rose from the ashes, and is now the official New Jersey State Theater.

Essex is urban, but it is far from an anachronism. Consider Newark, the most urban of all.

Anchored by the long-standing superiority of The Newark Public Library, the hub of regional library service in northern New Jersey; and the Newark Museum, recognized as probably the best small city museum in the nation, the city in 1995 experienced the excitement of a $150 million cultural center rising in the heart of a reviving downtown.

Consider, too, a college and university complex on the western hill, where forty thousand students attend classes; a world-class airport that is closer in both distance and time to the center of Manhattan than any other metropolitan airport; and a state-of-the-art seaport adjacent to the airport. This is also a city where the Ironbound section thrives and is noted for its fabled restaurants; where "North Newark" has neighborhoods as sound as ever; where the springtime cherry blossom show in Branch Brook Park in Newark and Belleville merits national attention; and where the nation's fifth largest cathedral invites awe.

The colonial heritage lives on, in luxuriously wide Broad Street, Washington, and Military parks laid out in 1666, and in

its two noted colonial churches, Old First, a block from the city center, and Trinity, at the north end of Military Park.

Downtown Newark is dominated by the scores of new high-rise office buildings erected since the 1967 turmoil, with more on the way. Affordable housing, public and private, is rising. Newark seemingly has in place most of the ingredients, not only for a return to pre-1960s stature but possibly as a showcase model for all of America's small cities.

Kenneth Gibson, elected in 1970 as the first African-American mayor of a major American City, often was quoted: "Wherever American cities are going, Newark will get there first." By extension, that could mean urban Essex County.

As the century was drawing to a close, it was not quite clear where Newark and Essex County were going, but the harbingers were bright and hopes were high. The future looked bright indeed.

The first major mall in Essex County was the Livingston Mall, built on seventy acres of former farmland at the corner of Eisenhower Parkway and South Orange Avenue. The Mall opened on August 1, 1972, and has since been totally rebuilt and refurbished. Courtesy the Newark Public Library.

When marchers headed north on Broad Street in May 1966, to hail the three-hundredth anniversary of Newark's founding, there was little external evidence to indicate that the city was filled with smoldering resentments that would erupt in a tragic riot a year later. As the "Landing of Robert Treat" floated by, the large, enthusiastic audience generally felt the year-long observance had been a huge success. Courtesy the Newark News.

(Facing page) Port Newark is known worldwide as a handler of cargo, but it has at times berthed passenger ships. This moody photograph taken on a rainy night in 1967 shows the President Garfield tied up in Newark after completing a world cruise. Prudential-Grace passenger ships also sailed from Newark. Courtesy the Newark Public Library.

On a Sunday morning stroll the day after four days of rioting ended in July 1967, a small boy stood in awe as he surveyed the wreckage of Manzi's Department Store. He could not understand or comprehend the cost: $10 million in property damage. Later that day, other young boys talked with a National Guardsman assigned on temporary duty in the riot area.

(Left) Courtesy the Newark News

(Below) Courtesy New Jersey Newsphotos

St. Joseph's Catholic Church in the heart of the riot zone lost most of its parishioners. Newark Community Corporation converted it in two restaurants, health centers, and a baby-keep-well center. The conversion showed as much as possible of the old church's architecture, stained glass windows, and wood enhanced by time. The cornerstone of the church was laid Thanksgiving Day, 1872. Courtesy New Jersey Newsphotos.

This handsome seven-story hospital is a centerpiece of the huge Newark campus of the New Jersey University of Medicine and Dentistry, built in the fire-scarred area where riots shocked the city in 1967. It is another of the mounting assets in a city rising on the ashes of the old. Courtesy the Newark Public Library.

Three East Orange Boy Scouts shoveled deep snow from the base of the city's imposing Lincoln statue in February 1969, in preparation for the annual commemoration of Lincoln's birthday. Courtesy the Newark Public Library.

Port Newark and Port Elizabeth combined in the 1970s to form a vast expanse of docking and storage space, and provided East Coast shippers with the most advanced equipment to load or unload containerized shipments. Huge quantities of automobiles, lumber, and hundreds of other products are imported or exported at these docks. The Port of New York and New Jersey Authority leases the facilities from Newark and Elizabeth. Courtesy the Port of New York and New Jersey Authority.

On April 27, 1994, Montclair State College officially became Montclair State University. Founded in 1908 as a two-year normal school, the university now is comprised of five schools, occupies a two-hundred-acre campus in Montclair, Little Falls, and Clifton, and has a student and faculty population of over 13,000. Courtesy Steve Hockstein, Harvard Studio, Montclair, New Jersey.

When the Wars of America monument was dedicated in Newark's Military Park, it memorialized veterans of all wars through World War I. Its meaning has been widened through the years to commemorate as well those who fought in World War II, the Korean War, Vietnam, and all the other conflicts in the nation's history. Courtesy New Jersey Newsphotos.

A helicopter view taken in 1988,
looking west over Newark,
features the many new buildings
that have risen in downtown
Newark since 1960, particularly
in the Gateway Center in the
foreground. The distinctive black
or white buildings intermingle
with taller buildings of the late
1920s and early 1930s. Courtesy
New Jersey Newsphotos.

One of the most rewarding areas
for school field trips is the Edison
Laboratory in West Orange.
The sixth grade pupils shown
here traveled nearly fifty miles
to see firsthand the impact that
Thomas Edison had on world
culture. They are gathered
in the Edison library. Courtesy
the Newark Public Library.

President Ronald Reagan, speaker at Seton Hall University's 1983 commencement, joined Seton Hall President Edward D'Alessio in joyful congratulations to beloved singer Pearl Bailey, recipient of an honorary degree at the graduation ceremony. Courtesy New Jersey Newsphotos.

Bishop Desmond Tutu, a Nobel Peace Prize Laureate, was welcomed to St. Peter's Church in Essex Fells in October 1984, a coup for one of the smallest communities in Essex County. Bishop Tutu was welcomed by the church rector, the Reverend David St. George, and Christine Barney, executive director of Newark Episcopal Diocese. Courtesy New Jersey Newsphotos.

(Facing page) Newark Public Library's interior, finished in 1901, remains one of the remarkable sights in Essex County. Based on Boston Public Library's noted architecture, the Newark Library revolves around open space that rises four flights, in the manner of a Florentine palace. On dedication day, internationally known Library Director John Cotton Dana exclaimed that only "a major city" would build a library in the exquisite fashion of this time-honored structure. Courtesy the Newark Public Library, photograph by George Hawley.

If every street is bathed in the warm glow of old-fashioned gas street lights, you are in Glen Ridge. This scene, taken in a 1984 snowstorm, gave the town a quaint holiday-greeting-card look. South Orange and East Orange also have a few gas-lit streets, but Glen Ridge is "Gas Light Town." Courtesy the Newark Public Library.

Empty seats are rare at the Papermill Playhouse in Millburn, New Jersey's State Theater, where the scenery, costumes, and performances win critical acclaim. Once one of Millburn's noted papermaking establishments, the structure opened in the 1930s as a pleasant regional theater. The gutting of the interior by fire in 1980 was a blessing in disguise. The theater was rebuilt in modern fashion, to reward persistently full-house audiences with topflight theater. Courtesy the Newark Public Library.

Newark's future and past unite in the $165 million New Jersey Performing Arts Center that is rising in the heart of downtown Newark. The center is being built close to the "landing place" on the Passaic River where Robert Treat and his Connecticut followers stepped ashore in May 1666. Opening night for the magnificent Great Hall (shown in an artist's conception), the center of the complex, is set for 1997. It will mark completion of the third largest arts center on the East Coast and will mean an economic boom for Essex County in addition to its social and cultural enhancements. Courtesy the New Jersey Performing Arts Center.

One of New Jersey's most compelling structures is Sacred Heart Cathedral in the northern part of Newark, on the edge of Branch Brook Park. Started in 1899, the two-spired stone church was not finished until 1954. Sacred Heart is the nation's fifth largest cathedral. Courtesy the Newark Public Library.

This is Essex County, or at least about half of it. On this clear day in 1980, the photographer looked westward toward Second Mountain (also known as Orange Mountain) on the far horizon. To the right is the Passaic River, the historic entrance to the county. The railroad in the foreground is Amtrak, the key to the Gateway Center. The compactness of Newark, still tied to streets laid down more than three hundred years ago, is evident. Beyond are the Oranges, Montclair, Verona, Glen Ridge, and other towns east of Second Mountain. Courtesy the Newark Public Library.

(Facing page) Time stood still for a few days in 1985 when skilled artisans painted the two-hundred-year-old face of the clock in the steeple of Bloomfield's Presbyterian Church. The Roman numerals and the minute dots were embellished with gold leaf, as were the hour and minute hands before they were returned to position. Courtesy New Jersey Newsphotos.

Newark Museum, founded by John Cotton Dana in 1909, now includes these three buildings on Washington Street. The museum underwent a $7 million rebuilding and refurbishing in the 1980s to enhance its long-standing reputation as one of the nation's superb small city museums. The wing shown here houses modern art. Courtesy the Newark Museum.

Parking lots and roadways at Newark International Airport were jammed with automobiles when this scene was recorded in mid-January, 1986. In becoming the area's second busiest airport (sometimes the busiest), the facility experiences the constant growth pains of all airports. The Port of New York and New Jersey Authority, which leases the airport from the city of Newark, added this monorail train in 1995 to ease transportation within the airport. Courtesy New Jersey Newsphotos.

(Facing page) Montclair long ago left behind its early reputation as a suburban backwater, but amidst its busy streets and population growth, the widely known Presby Memorial Iris Garden has added uniqueness and color to the Upper Montclair railroad station since 1927. The garden contains six thousand varieties and seventy thousand iris plants. Courtesy New Jersey Newsphotos.

Courtesy New Jersey Newsphotos

The oldest institution of its kind in the state, the New Jersey Historical Society (below) has been located in Newark since its founding in 1845. It moved into this new "uptown" building in 1931 after being in the heart of the city for eighty-six years. Its priceless collections are scheduled to be moved back downtown by the year 2000 or earlier. The new location will be in the Essex Club (shown above), once the most prestigious businessmen's club in New Jersey. The downtown site will place The Society close to Newark's other cultural institutions as well as to many corporate offices.

Courtesy the New Jersey Historical Society

Proud that many visitors are struck by its similarity in appearance to European villages, Maplewood residents point out that Maplewood Avenue is the only avenue named for its town that does not have a traffic light along its entire length. Equally, they are pleased that the street has had no new construction since the 1920s. Courtesy the Newark Public Library.

Several renovations and alterations at Short Hills Mall since its opening have continued its reputation as a chic rendezvous for shoppers and browsers. A favored meeting place is the tall wooden sculpture at one of the escalators. Numbers, from nine on the bottom to zero on top, carry the sculptor's message. Courtesy the Newark Public Library.

Cherry blossom time in Branch Brook Park, in Newark and Belleville, each April attracts many thousands of visitors, including wedding parties aware that the delicate blooms make the perfect backdrop for their finery. The trees were the gift of Mrs. Felix Fuld, sister of Louis Bamberger, among the greatest of Essex County benefactors. There are now more than 2,500 flowering trees, giving Branch Brook Park more trees and more varieties than found in Washington, D.C. Courtesy New Jersey Newsphotos.

The Newark Boys Chorus has its own school in downtown Newark, where boys are taught academic skills as well as music. The school director, Elizabeth Del Tufo, has arranged tours for the choir that have taken it throughout the United States as well as to Prague, the Czech Republic, China, and Australia. Courtesy the Newark Boys Chorus School.

Opened in 1939 by the Dominican Sisters as a small Catholic institution, Caldwell College was founded to provide a quality education for women. It has recently broadened its original policies greatly, including changing its basic philosophy by admitting male students. Caldwell College reaches out to surrounding Essex County communities by encouraging very young students to utilize its facilities, including its state-of-the-art television studios. Courtesy New Jersey Newsphotos.

Sarah Vaughan, a native of Newark, began singing in city choirs and became known as the nation's premier jazz singer whose wide vocal range often was startling. When she died on April 3, 1990, the City of Newark, Essex County, and the nation mourned. Newark now hosts one of the nation's largest jazz festivals and radio station WBGO is one of few stations that play jazz twenty-four hours a day. Courtesy Public Broadcasting Service.

A feature of the annual Cuban Independence Day parade in Newark is placing a floral tribute at the José Martí memorial plaque near Pennsylvania Station. Martí is remembered by Newark's significant Cuban population for leading the revolution in 1895 that led to Cuban independence from Spain. Courtesy New Jersey Newsphotos.

Dr. Natércia Teixeira, Consul-General of Portugal at Newark, New Jersey, addressing a meeting of downtown business people. More than 100,000 Portuguese-Americans are centered in and around Newark and throughout Essex County and the adjoining counties of Hudson and Union. Every year nearly a quarter million attend the community's annual Portugal Day parade in early June, marching up Newark's Ironbound main thoroughfare—Ferry Street. Courtesy Consul-General of Portugal.

The 1988–1989 Seton Hall University Basketball Team. First row, left to right: Manager Chris Crowell, Rene Monteserin, Gerald Greene, Khyiem Long, Daryll Walker, Ramon Ramos, John Morton, Pookey Wigington, Jose Rebimbas, and Manager Dave Flood. Second row, left to right: Assistant Coach John Carroll, Assistant Coach Rod Baker, Assistant Coach Bruce Hamburger, Trevor Crowley, Nick Katsikis, Frantz Volcy, Anthony Avent, Andrew Gaze, Michael Cooper, Assistant Coach Tom Sullivan, Trainer John Levitt, and Head Coach P. J. Carlesimo.

An ASPIRA dancer takes part in the twenty-eighth annual Puerto Rican State-wide Parade in downtown Newark in 1990. At present there are more than twenty Spanish-language groups including Puerto Ricans in the metropolitan Newark region. Courtesy of New Jersey Newsphotos.

ESSEX COUNTY
A SHORT READING LIST

Cunningham, John T. *Newark*. (Newark: New Jersey Historical
    Society. 2d ed. 1989) 384 pp.
    (The most modern complete one-volume history of
    New Jersey's largest city. A pleasant yet detailed
    narrative runs from the earliest settlers to present-day
    urban conditions. Two chapters have been added to
    update the original 1966 edition. Illustrated with
    hundreds of historical drawings and current photo-
    graphs.)

(Essex Co. N.J. Dept. of Planning-Economic Development
    Conservation)) *County Profile. History of Essex
    County.* (Newark, N.J.: na., 1976. 27 pp.
    (27-page typescript devoted to the development of
    Newark and suburban Essex communities with line
    drawings, and miscellaneous information on climate,
    rainfall, etc.)

Folsom, Joseph Fulford, ed. *The Municipalities of Essex
    County, New Jersey. 1664–1924. (*New York: Lewis
    Historical Publishing Company, Inc. 1925.
    (Vols I and II contain general history, institutions (ie
    education, churches, medical history etc.), and
    histories of towns excluding Newark. Vols III and IV
    contain individual biographies.)

Goldberg, Barbara. *The History of Essex County, New Jersey, 1664–1970.* (n.p. no pub. n.d.) 25 pp.

(A short 25-page five-era mimeographed history of Essex County, beginning with the Proprietors and ending with the 1970s.)

Marucci, Leonard. *Essex County: A Profile and Scenic Tour.* (West Orange, N.J.: no pub., 1978.) 48 pp.

(Conceived as a "pictorial profile" which might awaken the curiosity of the residents of Essex County. The author is interested in heritage, houses of worship, famous people, and general development of the county, as well as an updated economic profile for the the late 1970s.)

New Jersey Bell. Urban Affairs Dept. *A Profile of New Jersey. Essex County.* (Newark N.J.: New Jersey Bell, 1979.)

(Statistical background of each of the county's 22 municipalities. Census data includes real estate property values, housing statistics, water regulations, crime, education, industrial and business property taxes, along with telephone statistics.)

The Oranges and Their Leading Business Men, Embracing Those of Orange, Brick Church, East Orange, West Orange, South Orange, and Orange Valley. (Newark N.J.: Mercantile Publishing Company, 1890.) 103 pp.

(103-page history and classified list of local businesses.)

Shaw, William H. comp. *History of Essex and Hudson Counties, New Jersey.* (Philadelphia: Everts and Peck, 1884.) 2 vols. 1332 pp.

(The first and most complete history ever written of

Essex and Hudson Counties, and one that served as a model for later county histories. Chapters include general history from the earliest settlers to the time of publication; also business and industry, agriculture, transportation, public works, and many other such topics, and several hundred biographies of prominent people of the time. Many excellent drawings and portraits are included with the text.)

This Is Essex County/Prepared by the League of Women Voters of Essex County. (Newark, N.J.): The League (1981). 50 pp.
(A publication designated "to help the Citizens understand the structure, function, and services of county government, as well as the history of our county". . . a handy reference tool. . . . In addition to brief descriptions of county government agencies, the publication includes a list of historic sites, an enumeration of famous residents, and miscellaneous facts relating to Essex County.)

Urquhart, Frank. *A History of the City of Newark, New Jersey. Embracing Practically Two and a Half Centuries, 1666–1913.* New York: Lewis Historical Publishing Co., New York, 1913 (3 vols.)
(A two volume history of Newark, N.J. from the time of its founding until the eve of the 250th anniversary celebration in 1916. While it is strictly a history of Newark it also includes earlier portions of Newark, later part of Essex County and beyond its present boundaries. Volume 3 is devoted to the typical turn-of-the-century biographical sketches.)

We gratefully recognize a wide variety of Essex County people who have aided us in putting together Remembering Essex, particularly those individuals who have assisted us in securing illustrations. The quality of the book will speak for itself through both words and pictures, but the authors accept responsibility for any errors in caption information or other data. We have listed those who have given assistance alphabetically; the position in the list therefore is not necessarily indicative of the magnitude of the contribution.

Hope Alswang, Director, The New Jersey
    Historical Society
Mr. and Mrs. Wilmot Bartle
Ronald Becker, Head, Archives and
    Special Collections-Rutgers
The Belleville Public Library
Robert Blackwell, The Newark Public
    Library
Mr. and Mrs. Antonio Braga, The Newark
    Public Library
David S. Bryant
Richard Cass
Jack Chance, The Montclair Historical
    Society
Andrea Cohen, The Belleville Public
    Library
William Cone, Photographer
Sylvella Copeland, The Newark Public
    Library
Emily Curry
Ellen B. Defranco
Charles DeMarco
Margaret DiSalvi, The Newark Museum
Harry Dorer, Photographer
Lesley Douthwaite, The Morristown-
    Morris Township Free Public
    Library
The East Orange Public Library
Mark Eisen, East Orange Public Library
The Glen Ridge Public Library
Richard Grossklaus
D. J. and Elizabeth Henderson
Robert Holton
The Irvington Public Library
Dorothy Johnson, The Bloomfield Public
    Library
Dorothy Jones, The East Orange Public
    Library
Donald Karp, Broad National
    Bancorporation

Richard Kole, NJ Newsphotos
Emily Matonti, The Newark Public
    Library
Lorelei McConnell
Mark Meyers, Researcher
The Montclair Historical Society
The Montclair Public Library
Montclair State University
New Jersey Division, The Newark Public
    Library
The New Jersey Historical Society
New Jersey Newsphotos
The New Jersey Performing Arts Center
    of Newark
The Newark Evening News
The Newark Museum
The Newark Sunday News
Msgr. William Noefield
Jeff Norman, NJ-PAC
Dr. John E. O'Conner
Princeton University Archives
The Roseland Historical Society
Rutgers-Archives and Special
    Collections
Louis Schindell
Seton Hall University
Deborah Smith, The Morristown-Morris
    Township Free Public Library
Diana St. Lifer, Montclair State
    University
Dr. Paul Stellhorn, The Newark Public
    Library
Dr. Natércia Teixeira, Consul General of
    Portugal
Gail Thompson, NJ-PAC
Jean-Rae Turner, NJ Newsphotos
The West Caldwell Public Library
Howard Wiseman, The Newark Public
    Library

John T. Cunningham, author of 34 books and more than 2,000 magazine articles on his native state, has been called "New Jersey's popular historian" by the New Jersey Historical Commission and "Mr. New Jersey" by Rutgers University when it awarded him an honorary degree. He recently spanned a wide spectrum of history as acting curator for an exhibit on baseball at the New Jersey State Museum and through publication of the Fourth Edition of his state classic, *This is New Jersey*, by Rutgers University Press. Nearly all of his books have been embellished by numerous photographs and other illustrative materials, as is the case with *Remembering Essex County*.

Charles F. Cummings, long respected as one of New Jersey's leading librarians, also is valued as one of the state's most vital personages in historical research. In the former role, he led a dedicated staff in making the New Jersey Division of The Newark Public Library one of the most valued local history resources in the nation. In his other role, hundreds of individual researchers and myriads of historical societies, corporations, and municipalities know that the words "service" and "accuracy" are Cummings' hallmarks. He practices what he preaches as the official historian of the City of Newark. Cummings is co-author of several books, numerous articles and bibliographies; has edited a newspaper column; and has produced a subject index for the *Newark Star-Ledger* since 1970. As part of his interest in historical preservation, his chief interest has been the development of picture sources and collections. Some of his own photographs are in this volume, mostly credited to Newark Public Library.